Dieter Graf

Rhodes
Karpathos
Kos
Southern
Dodecanese

Chálki
Kárpathos & Saría
Kássos
Kastellórizo
Kós
Nísyros
Psérimos
Rhodes
Sími
Tílos

Hiking and Swimming for Island-Hoppers
50 Walks on Ten Greek Islands

Graf Editions

Using this illustrated walking guide

AWT stands for Actual Walking Time. This time does not include breaks, wrong turns or sight-seeing. The AWT serves as a personal control as to whether certain route markings, emphasized in **bold print**, have been reached in the given time. These times are an aid for orientation and should not be considered as encouragement to achieve a record performance. Spot heights are added in brackets.

The approximate **overall length** of a walk is specified in hours in the introduction to each tour. These figures do not include time taken for bus trips or extra-long breaks. Information concerning the **length of the walks**, the **difference in altitude** and three **levels of difficulty** can also be found there.

Route photos are intended for orientation, for consulting locals and as a stimulus. The corresponding text is marked by ① to ④. The **route sketches** have been drawn to the best of our knowledge but lay no claim to completeness.

GPS points are shown as P in texts and on maps. Map datum WGS84.

We would be grateful for useful information concerning **changes** in paths and similar data. As a token of our appreciation we will send you a free copy of our next edition.

The website www.graf-editions.de informs you of any changes that occur along walking routes.

The author **Dieter Graf** is an architect who has travelled all over the world. He has walked the Aegean Islands since the years when tourism was just beginning there and is considered a connoisseur of the islands.

© 2011 Edition Dieter Graf, Elisabethstr. 29, 80796 Munich, Germany
    Tel. 0049-(0)89-271 59 57, Fax 0049-(0)89-271 59 97
    www.graf-editions.de

Type-Setting: Michael Henn, Reichenschwand · Maps: Kurt Zucher, Wielenbach
Translation: Myles Oliver, Muenchen

Original Title: Wandern auf Griechischen Inseln: Rhodos, Karpathos, Kos, Südlicher Dodekanes (ISBN 978-3-9814047-0-8)

Cover photo: Kássos

ISBN 978-3-9814047-1-5

Contents

Tips for Walks *6*
Landscape, Flora, Fauna *10*
History *15*
Walks *20*
Translation helper F, I, NL, S *86*
Helpful Greek Words *173*
Explanation of Symbols *176*

Akramitis

Rhodes and the Dodecanese Islands

The Dodecanese archipelago stretches 160 km along the west coast of Turkey from Pátmos to Rhodes. The name is made up of "dodéka" meaning twelve and "nísos" island: the group of twelve islands. A few smaller islands have been added to this group so that meanwhile there are 25 inhabited islands in the "group of twelve". Altogether there are even 163 islands and islets. In this book the ten southern inhabited islands are described.

The Dodecanese Islands are characterised by an enormous variety, not only with regard to landscape but also culturally. The visitor will find wide sandy dunes, small rocky bays, shady pine forests, extinguished volcanoes and thousand meter high mountains. If you are interested, you can view the evidence of a rich cultural history on these old islands on the point of intersection with the Orient: ancient temples, fortresses from the crusades, Oriental mosques and medieval towns.

On top of that comes the original Greek nature, the friendly people and their hospitality, filoxenía. In Greek "xenos" means "stranger" and "guest" simultaneously. Away from the tourist areas this hospitality can still be encountered, especially in remote regions off the beaten track, regions which sometimes it is only possible to reach on foot.

This book should help you to find the loveliest of the authentic old mule tracks which will lead you to hidden cloisters closely-knit mountain villages and to wonderful isolated bathing beaches. This extended and improved edition of the hiking guide provides not just text, maps and photos of the trails, but also GPS data for better orientation. All the tours were walked again and updated before going to press.

While walking, you can rediscover the beauty of slowness and enjoy the variety of the islands with all your senses: the smell of thyme, the clear ringing of the goats' bells, the freshness of clear spring water, the manifold colours of the spring blossoms and especially the friendliness of the people

Have a good trip!   *Kaló taxídi!*

Walking on the Dodecanese Islands

The Dodecanese Islands are, thanks to their position in front of the mountains of Asia Minor, blessed with sufficient precipitation. The vegetation is correspondingly luscious, making the islands an ideal hiking region. Moreover, the hiker still finds many intact **old mule tracks.** For centuries these narrow *monopátia* used to help the farmers work the fields and, up until 30 years ago, formed a dense network of tracks (photo p. 118). By contrast, the up to four metre wide paved tracks, the *kalderímia,* connected larger villages for the transport of goods and served as paths for pilgrims to the monasteries. They were paved with marble and bordered with walls. Some of them are said to be up to 1000 years old.

Motorisation has not failed to leave its mark on the islands either. Instead of mules the farmers now use pickups, which require wider roadways. The old network of tracks was torn apart by broadening the mule tracks to make them accessible to cars wherever it seemed to be necessary and by pushing aside the characteristic dry walls along the waysides, all co-financed by money from the European Union Regional Funds. The remaining paths are now superfluous and in ruins and are gradually being forgotten by the islanders. Lately, however, the EU Leader Fund provides money to restore some of the remaining mule tracks, mainly for the sake of tourism. Instead of maintaining and extending the scope of the network, however, this often only amounts to the over-perfect restoration of individual paths. This book aims to help ensure that the old mule tracks which still exist are used again and hence preserved before they are irreparably destroyed. They may, above all in spring, be rather overgrown!

The routes described have been walked along again shortly before publication and can be followed without difficulty by people in normal physical condition. Some of the walks are suitable for children. Special surefootedness is not necessary. The ✓ markings in the text concern only those who are very afraid of heights. For longer walking tours **short cuts** are indicated. Due to the good views, the tours normally lead from the mountains to the sea – so take along your swimming gear. You should be absolutely sure to pick a nice day for tours in the mountains since there is always the danger of sudden fog formation. Moreover it can rain there even in summer. On the other hand there is a risk of bush fires in the summer.

If you want to walk alone, you should by all means leave information in your hotel and save the number of the hotel on your mobile phone. In order to get your blood circulation going, you should begin leisurely for the first fifteen minutes and, during the tour, eat and especially drink often, even if you don't feel the need to do so. The route maps show springs and wells to be found by the wayside. Be sure to protect yourself sufficiently against sun and wind too.

Coloured dots and arrows can often be found as **markings along paths**, but they do not necessarily correspond to the descriptions in this book. In addition there are the wooden signs and little red-and-white metal signs of the Greek organisations. Above all on Kárpathos and Tílos the old network of paths is now being marked and maintained.

There are road maps for a few islands and, recently, **walking maps** too, for example from the Austrian Kompass-Verlag or the Greek Anavasi publishing house.

As new roadways continue to be built, it may be that the route descriptions are partly out of date, thus calling for certain **orientation skills.** If you have orientation problems, you should always ask the locals about the "monopáti", otherwise you will be directed to roads for vehicular traffic. Mule dung on the narrow paths is more certain to lead you further than goat droppings since the goat paths usually end somewhere in the scrub, while mules always return to their stalls. If you lose your way, you may have to shin up a field wall or climb over steel mesh used as grazing fences with the help of a pile of stones. Some pasture fences are knotted shut on the side where there are two perpendicular rods. You owe it to the farmers whose land you walk across to shut the openings again afterwards, of course. Access to the sea is allowed in Greece as a matter of principle.

Despite efforts, environmental protection still remains an unsolved problem, so some things you see lying around while walking through the countryside will not always correspond to your sense of order and environmental stipulations.

Almost all the starting and finishing points are served by public buses, even in the low season. In case a service does not operate, take a taxi. You should always make a point of settling the price before you begin the trip. The taximeter is only turned on when you specifically request it. A possibility for circular walking tours is a relatively reasonable rental car or a rental motor bike. In addition, car drivers also enjoy taking along a wanderer who waves him down.

Sufficient **wandering gear** includes a backpack for a day, shoes with good soles (no sandals), comfortable socks, long trousers or zipper trousers*, a mobile phone possibly, binoculars, a whistle, a small flashlight and picnic equipment with a salt-shaker. In the spring and fall, rain gear is a necessity. A GPS device or a compass would also be good but is not necessary if you have a somewhat good sense of orientation.

*The legs of zipper trousers which also have vertical zippers can be zipped together to form a pad to sit on at the beach. And if you connect both zippers, you have a chic skirt for visiting monasteries.

Climate and Walking Season

The typical, temperate Mediterranean climate with a hot summer and mild, rainy winter predominates on the Dodecanese. The maximum **air temperature** is 32 °C in August (at night 22 °C). In the winter the temperature sinks to 15 °C (7 °C) in February. Snow can fall every 3–4 years in the mountains over 1000 m high and lie there for a short while.

The **water temperatures** are lowest in February at 16 °C and reach an almost subtropical 25 °C in August. You can go swimming from the end of May at 19 °C through October (22 °C).

The mountains in Asia Minor help the islands located in front of them to get more **rain** than is found in the more western Cyclades. However, the rainy days are strewn irregularly throughout the year. Most of the rain falls in December and January, when it rains on about 14 days. You must still calculate with 3 days of rain in May, while there is absolute dryness from June to August. Statistically October has 6 days of rain again, but it is not very plentiful.

The number of **hours of sun** per day corresponds to this. In December and January the very strong winter sun shines only about 4.5 hours. Even in May the wanderer must reconcile himself to 10.1 hours of sun daily and the swimmer in August to 12.1. October is pleasant for autumn walkers once again, with 7.8 hours of sun per day.

Strong **north winds** are characteristic of the Aegean Islands, with three to four Beaufort on a yearly average. One reason for this is the air pressure difference between the Azore highs and the hot low pressure areas above the Persian Gulf. In the transition season, especially in April and May and then October and November, the Boréas dominates, a cool, wet north wind. In the summer, mainly between May and September, the famous etesien winds, called the meltémia (from the Turkish word "meltem", the breeze) often blow for days under a cloudless blue sky, regularly strong from north to northeast, with velocities of five to six Beaufort. The sky can then be somewhat overcast. Towards evening the meltémi usually slackens somewhat, but it can also blow with quite great strength for days on end.

The schirókko occurs less frequently, but especially in the spring. It comes from the hot Sahara desert, picks up moisture over the Mediterranean to bring the Aegean warm humidity from the south.

On the Greek islands there are several different **seasons for walking tours.** Anyone wanting to give his eyes a treat should plan his tour around Easter. It might be somewhat cool and even muddy, but the countryside is grass-green, poppy-red and broom-yellow; the houses and alleyways are freshly white-washed. Even just the preparations for the Greek Easter celebration are worth the trip. However, you can't go swimming yet, and some hotels and tavernas are still closed. In April it can rain at the spur of a moment. The Greeks divide the year in three parts, and this one is called "the time blossoming and maturing".

In May and June the blossom time is already partially over, but, since it is very warm and the number of tourists is still limited, this is probably the loveliest time for walking. Beginning at the end of May the water has a pleasant temperature.

The main tourist season in July and August is not highly recommended for walking tours due to the heat. It is the "dry period" in Greece. The north winds, which blow consistently, still make the temperatures bearable, but at noon a shady spot under a tree is advisable. Harvest time begins in July. On August 15, the Assumption of the Virgin, in the eastern church called "Passing Away Peacefully", there are great celebrations everywhere with roast lamb, music and dance.

From the beginning of September on, the heat is over and the sea still has a pleasant temperature for swimming until the end of October. Now longer walking tours can be taken once again, but only until about 6 p.m. due to the shorter period of daylight. The land has become yellow and brown, the fields bear their fruit, and everywhere you meet friendly farmers harvesting their last crops. Starting at the beginning of October it can start to rain again. The restaurants and hotels gradually shut down, and some owners travel to their winter residences in Athens. Others put on camouflage suits, reach for their guns and search through the brush. A million Greeks are passionate hunters. In November there is usually a change in climate, with heavy rainfall. Then it becomes unpleasant. The period from November to February is called the "rain season". Although there are some warm, sunny days around Christmas, it is more pleasant at home.

Geology

Two different types of geological origin have been established. The **northern Dodecanese islands** are shelf islands. They rise 100 to 200 metres out of the submarine Asiatic continental base, the shelf, and were separated from the Asian continent as the geological history of the earth developed. The northern Aegean was not flooded by the sea until after the last ice age. After various actions of rising and falling, the islands took on their present form. Several volcanoes have broken through the shelf, as on Nísyros or Kós. The floor of the sea falls down to 1000 m towards the west and forms the geological border to Europe.

On the other hand, **Rhodes and Kárpathos** together with Crete form a broad arc of islands extending from Asia Minor to the Peloponnes. These islands rise up from underwater calcareous (chalky) mountains which fall off sideways to a level of 2500 metres under the water. They originated 50 million years ago through the pressure exerted by the African continental plate onto the European. The highest mountains in the Aegean rise up along this backbone of islands: the Atáviros on Rhodes (1215 m), the Kalilímni on Kárpathos (1214 m) and the Ida, which towers 2456 m above Crete.

Fauna

Larger wild animals are not present - due to the mostly small-sized vegetation. It is only on Rhodes that there have been roe deer since antique times; these were bred again by the Italians. As a result of the mostly low vegetation large game is not encountered. Hares and martens are seldom. The animals one most often comes across are goats and sheep, though not in such large numbers as in former years. Sometimes even pasture land is burned off, in order to create fresh nutriments for goats. The few cows have an almost exotic charm.

Of the smaller animals one hears and sees the small common lizard, which can be up to 10 cm long. The dragon-like agama (hardun) ①), its bigger relative, is up to 30 cm long. Even land turtles have now become rare.

The careful wanderer will rarely see snakes. There is only one poisonous type: the horn or sand viper ②. It can be up to 50 cm long and as thick as two thumbs. A healthy adult hardly need fear a deadly bite.

The non-poisonous sand-boa is about the same size. The non-poisonous four-striped-adder reaches an adult length of more than a metre and a width almost as thick as an arm. Its size is frightening, but it is harmless, as is the ring-snake. As long as one does not move completely silently, the snakes disappear again. Long trousers give additional protection. On no account should one lift up large stones, as snakes may be sleeping underneath them.

The up to 5 cm long scorpions also hide there. The bite of a scorpion is rather painful but not deadly. They also love to hide in shoes.

You can rouse crabs, frogs and eels along the watercourses. In rocky bays you should look out for sea urchins ③.

Soaring above in search of prey are birds such as buzzards, falcons and griffon vultures; unfortunately migratory birds often fall victim to the Greek passion for hunting.

Flora

The islands of the Dodecanese are mainly green and fertile since the clouds collect in the mountains of Asia Minor and bring greater amounts of rain in winter. Pine forests ① however are only to be found on the larger islands, for ever since antiquity forests on the Aegean islands have been cut down for building ships or have fallen victim to forest fires in summer, causing some parts of the countryside to seem like karstland. This effect is intensified by the limestone soil which cannot store water. Nevertheless, along with Spain, Greece has the greatest variety of plants in Europe.

The **stock of trees** consists mainly solitary specimens. Taller evergreen oaks and kermes oaks ② grow in protected regions which are rich in water. Unassuming, salt-tolerant tamarisks ③ are found along beaches. Plane-trees ④ shade the village squares and slender cypresses the cemeteries. Acacias, poplars, alders, maples and eucalyptus trees ⑤ can also be found, as well as mulberry trees ⑥ and carobs ⑦. Among the fruit trees there are pomegranates, fig trees ⑧ and citrus fruits. Yet dominating the

landscape most of all is the olive tree, which looks strangely deformed as it gets older.

In the open countryside dry shrubs reaching a height of up to half a metre predominate, thorny undergrowth (garrigue) called **phrýgana** in Greek. Typical representatives of this "low macchia" are broom, thorny knap-weed, heather, spiny spurge plants (euphorbia) ⑨ ⑩, plants often shaped like hedgehogs. Jerusalem sage, squill and asphodel ⑪ blossom there.

Thicker bush or tree groups up to two metres high with evergreens and bushes with hard leaves are not found as frequently. This "high macchia" is called **xerovoúmi** in Greek. Kermes oaks with serrated leaves ② , juniper and mastic bushes ⑫ are particularly predominant.

The agave ⑬, attributed to the cactus family, often lines the lanes and paths. This thorny leaf plant has only grown in the Mediterranean area since the 16th century. The fruit of the fig-cactus ⑭ makes a sweet supplement to any hiker's picnic.

Flowers can mainly be appreciated in spring. Already in January the anemone and crocus blossom. Then, from February through

to May/June, all the splendour of white and red blossoming rockroses ⑮,), iris, yellow daffodils, hyacinths, lupines, chrysanthemums and broom add magic to the landscape with their cheery colours, and the poppy adds its bright red.

Small **orchids** are an adornment of spring for a short time. The bee orchid (ophrys) ⑯, lax-flowered orchid (orchis), tongue orchid (serapias) and dragon arum ⑰ can be seen frequently.

In May and June the main blossoming season comes to an end, but summer doesn't mean brown wilderness by any means. Bougainvillea radiates its bright colours on the house walls, and oleander blossoms in moist spots. The thorny acanthus ⑱ and the gold thistle ⑲ bloom along the wayside. When the summer heat subsides, meadow-saffron, heather and squill reveal themselves along with the dandelions, thistles and cyclamen.

Sage ⑳, capers ㉑ and other kitchen herbs often border the walking paths. While walking you can especially appreciate the pleasantly spicy aroma of thyme, rosemary, lavender, oregano, camomile and fennel. Cultivated in the coastal plains are potatoes, wheat and vegetables. And, of course wine.

A brief history

Prehistoric Period   The first traces of mankind on Rhodes date back to around 5000 BC. The islands' position between Europe and Asia soon makes them a bridge between the two cultures and one of the oldest landscapes in Europe to be cultivated by man from a very early age.

The first immigrants, the Carians, come from Asia Minor around 2800 BC. Four thousand years ago the Phoenicians arrive from the coast of what is now Lebanon. They impart the skills of the Assyrians and Babylonians to the Greeks, as well as introducing writing and money.

Then the islands come under the influence of Minoan Crete. After the downfall of Crete's palaces around 1400 BC, Minoan settlers land and give the impulse for the first blossoming of culture here. Around 1200 BC these settlements are, however, relinquished. Starting in 1500 BC, the Achaeans immigrate from the Peloponnes. After 1100 BC the Aegean islands and Asia Minor are colonised in several waves by peoples from Greece.

Archaic Period   (700–490 BC) The Ionians dominate on the northern Dodecanese; south of the island of Léros the Spartan Dorians prevail. Here the Rhodian city of Líndos soon attains outstanding importance. From Rhodes, colonies as far as in Sicily and Spain are founded. In the 8th century the "Hexapolis" is formed, a league of three of Rhodes' city-states with Kós as well as Knidos and Halikarnass in Asia Minor.

Starting in 540 BC, the Persian Empire extends its influence to the coast of Asia Minor. Thereupon the Greeks of the Aegean and Asia Minor join forces with Athens to form the Athenian-Delian League. The island of Délos becomes the intellectual and cultural centre of this protective alliance. The Persian Wars are inevitable and begin in 490 BC.

The Classical Period   (490–336 BC) The Dorian islands fight on the side of the enemy at the beginning of the Persian Wars, but they, too, are on Athens' side for the final triumph over the Persians in 449 BC. Immense riches are amassed on Délos during the Golden Age which follows.

When Athens carries off the treasure and tries to make vassals of its allies, they fight in the Peloponnesian War in alliance with Sparta against, but also partly with Athens. The outcome is a forever weakened Greece. Athens loses all its importance, but the newly founded city of Rhodes, with 80,000 inhabitants, is soon one of the richest in the world at that time.

Hellenistic Period (338–146 BC) The Macedonians in northern Greece take over the Greek culture after conquering Greece in 338 BC and then shortly afterwards the islands. For a short period Alexander the Great, a Macedonian, takes this culture, henceforth known as "Hellenism", as far as India. Under his successors Rhodes strengthens its power. Sculptures from Rhodes attain a world-wide reputation; the Colossus of Rhodes, 30 m high, is created. Along with Alexandria, Rhodes is the most important city in the Mediterranean.

Roman Period (146 BC–330 AD) After 146 BC the Romans, as the next rulers, also make the Greek culture their own, thus helping its spread throughout Europe. The Greek culture becomes that of the Occident.

Important Romans visit the Dodecanese, either as visitors at the health resorts of the Asklipieion on Kós or as scholars at the school of rhetoric on Rhodes, among them Caesar, Cicero, Cassius, Cato, Brutus, Tiberius and Pompey. In 51 AD the apostle Paul travels through the islands, which have very early contact to Christianity, which also becomes the state religion in Eastern Roman Empire (Byzantine Empire) in 391 AD. When Délos becomes a free port, the economic importance of Rhodes comes to an end.

The Byzantine Period (330–1204 AD) While the Western Roman Empire is declining during the migration of peoples in 476 AD, the eastern part of the Imperium Romanum remains an upholder of Graeco-Roman culture for another 1000 years. Byzantium, the second Rome, turns eastwards, brings Christianity to the Slavs and spreads Greek ideas as far as Moscow, which later becomes known as the Second Byzantium or Third Rome. The new Islamic ideas also influence Greece in the 8th and 9th centuries. In the feud over pictures, iconoclasm, the admissibility of a pictorial representation of God and the Saints is disputed.

Europe begins to drift apart in cultural terms; the religious differences also deepen. It is disputed whether the Holy Ghost only emanates from God the Father or also from his Son, as the Roman Catholic Church believes. Another controversy is the corporal ascension of Mary, which is considered as a "peaceful passing away" in the Orthodox Church. In 1054 the schism or final separation of the Eastern Greek-Orthodox Church from the Western Latin Church of Rome comes about.

In these uncertain times the Aegean Islands are often attacked and occupied by the Vandals, Goths, Normans and then the Saracens. The inhabitants of the islands withdraw into the mountain villages. It isn't until the 9th century that Byzantium can consolidate its power once again. Now, however, in the wake of the Persians, Avars, Arabs and Seljuks, a new great Asian power has assembled on the eastern borders of Byzantium: the Turkish Ottoman Empire. It pushes westward with immense force. In 1095 the Eastern Roman Empire requests help from Pope Urban II, and the crusades begin. They are a fiasco. Jerusalem, which has been a place of pilgrimage until now, cannot be held on by the Christians. During the fourth crusade, one of the most short-sighted campaigns in history is initiated. Due to trade rivalries, Venice induces the crusaders to plunder the Byzantine capital, Constantinople, in 1204. The quadriga on San Marco square is one part of the loot. Byzantium is too weak to ever recover again and is conquered by the Turks in 1453.

Venetian Period and Order of St. John of Jerusalem   (1204–1523)
For most of the Dodecanese islands the Sack of Constantinople is followed first by Venetian, then Genoese rule. In 1309 Genoa sells the larger islands to the St. John's Order which has been expelled from Jerusalem but some of whom also, as in the case of Rhodes, forcefully expel the nominal owner Byzantium. The Order of St. John seeks to defend Christianity from here, even by means of piracy. It turns Rhodes into its power base and develops the city into the strongest fortress in Europe.

The Ottoman Empire directs all its energy to conquering Europe. Already in 1480 Rhodes is besieged without success for the first time. After the mightiest fortress of the Occident then finally falls in 1523, the Turks push further west. Not until Vienna and Malta can the Pope's "Holy League" halt their triumphal march.

The Turkish Era   (1523–1912) The Fall of Constantinople in 1453 marks the end of the thousand-year-old advanced Greek civilisation. Learned Byzantine fugitives bring the Greek way of thinking back to the West once again, paving the way for the Renaissance. From this time on, the fortune of the Orthodox Church is determined in Moscow, which also assumes the Byzantine double-headed eagle and the Roman Imperial claim for power.

Yet the whole of Greek life, from music to diet, is dominated by

Turkish influence for the next 350 years. This influence is still recognisable to a degree today. There is somewhat greater freedom on the islands, but this always depends on the current representative of the "Sublime Porte" in Istanbul. The Orthodox Church proves to be the safeguard of Greek culture. Children are taught the Greek language and writing in secret schools.

Independent Greece (since 1821) Finally, at the beginning of the 19th century, Europe reflects on its cultural roots. The political stability of post-Napoleonic Europe and Classicism in art increase awareness of eastern Europe. Philhellenists from many countries support the Greek struggle for independence after 1821, the Great Powers in Europe help diplomatically, and Greece becomes a part of Europe again.

However, not the islands in front of the Turkish coast. The London Protocol of 1830 regulates the new order in the Aegean area and determines their continued dependence on Turkey. There is only greater autonomy in administration.

The Italian Dodecanese (1912–1947) Italy, which has come too late for dividing up his part of the world, begins a successful war against Turkey in North Africa in 1911 and helps itself to a part of the "sick man on the Bosporus". Following this there is a Greek uprising on the Dodecanese. The Turks leave the islands, and the Italians appear here as the new masters. The Dodecanese are later integrated into Mussolini's new Imperium Romanum as "Italian possessions in the Aegean". After his end, German troops occupy them from 1943 until the end of the war. "Ennosis", the late return to the fatherland, finally takes place in 1947, after a brief period of British administration. In a plebiscite the population decided to become Greek again, after over 700 years, rather than join the British Commonwealth.

After World War II With Western help during the civil war from 1945 to 1949, Greece avoids the fate of the other Balkan countries, and doesn't disappear behind the Iron Curtain. Gradually Greece is accepted in the most important European institutions. European subventions lead to an improvement in the infrastructure and help tourism to develop. This becomes the most important economic sector in the country. In 2002, the drachma, the oldest currency in the world, is replaced by the euro. Economic problems make it necessary for Europe to step in with more assistance in 2010.

Kástro Kritiniás

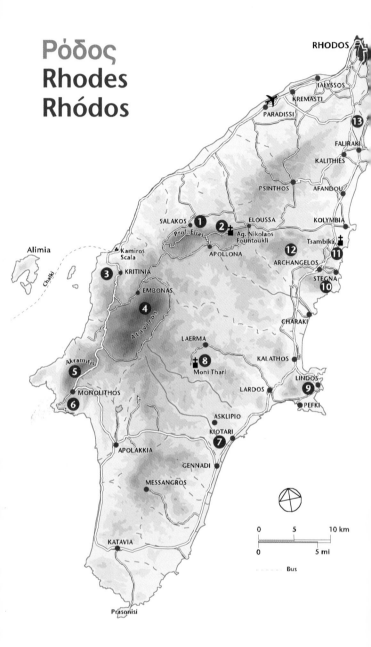

Ρόδος
Rhodes
Rhódos

Even in Roman times there was active tourism on this age-old island, pampered by the sun and brimming with culture. Refined Roman families sent their sons to the rhetoric school of Poseidonios on the "Rose Island".

Today Rhodes, with over a million visitors, is the most touristic island in the Aegean apart from Crete. This tourism, however, is concentrated on the beaches in the north.

After visiting the picturesque medieval old town, a world culture heritage site, the connoisseur of nature and landscape quickly moves on to the middle of the island.

Tourism hasn't established itself everywhere here yet. You can wander through pristine woods and mountains and discover chapels with important frescoes here and there. Yet there is no need to give up beaches.

Due to its great supplies of water, the island is green and fertile. A relief map of the island shows a mountainous spine parallel to the coast in the western part. It is dominated by the 1215 metre Mount Atáviros, the highest mountain in the Dodecanese. To the east and south of it, wooded hillsides spread out. Far to the south the landscape becomes flat and less spectacular. Here scrub dominates the vegetation.

A rental car is the easiest means of getting to various walks. Frequent bus connections are only available on the east side of the island, where Lindos, a lovely but crowded town, is a good base for walkers.

In the western part it is best to spend the night in the unspoilt mountain villages. Apart from the morning bus along the coast to Ancient Kameiros the bus service to here only operates in the afternoon.

Good road maps with data for walkers can be purchased from ReiseKnowHow, tc travel maps, Freytag&Berndt and Road Editions. The Austrian Kompass Verlag published a detailed map at a scale of 1:50 000 in 2009.

In the present book tours ①, ④, ⑤, ⑨ and ⑩ are particularly recommended. Starting out from Rhodes you can also take walking excursions to the neighbouring islands, Chálki and Sími.

❶ Alpine Chalets on Mount Elías

This four to five-hour mountain trek leads steeply, but wonderfully, up from the village of Sálakos to the state guest houses of the former Italian administration and further to the Profítis Elías.

Though unspoilt by tourism, Sálakos has good bus connections. It is, however, worth thinking about spending the night there and enjoying the delightful atmosphere of dinner next to the babbling fountain.

■ *9 km, difference in alt. 510 m, moderate to difficult*

AWT 0.00	At the village square in **Sálakos** (230 m) go 500 m along the slightly rising street to a right curve with a **little bus stop** and turn left at the sign "footpath". After walking
0.05 !!	100 m along the street, turn up to the right onto a **path** (also signposted). *Ten metres before a wayside shrine* turn left and, in spring, walk upwards through a rich green landscape. The zigzag path is partly shaded by kermes oaks and offers the wanderer an array of blossoms, de-
★	pending on the season – peonies, violets and even orchids ①. Despite the many spots of colour from the flowers, remember to pay attention to the dotted red path markings.
0.35	Once you have the steep part of the **ascent behind you** (**P1**: N36°16.833'/E27°56.828', 560 m), you see the antennas and enter the pine forest on level ground. After two

minutes, in an opening up to the right between the trees, the St. Michael Chapel comes into view. It is best not to head for it without a path (as signposted), but wait until the way runs 50 m past it.

From the chapel head for the wide path, where you turn left onto a marked footpath. This brings you to two dilapidated houses (left) and further right,

0.50 up to the two **hotels** ② (605 m).

> *These guest houses, named after the heraldic animals of Rhodes, the stag and the hind (elafas and elafína), were*

built in 1929 during the time of the Italian administration. The governor of the Dodecanese, the "Italian possessions in the Aegean", spent the hot season here, when the heat was too oppressive down in the town. After the war the complex fell into disrepair, but has been used again as a smart hotel since 2006. It is a popular meeting place for local high society.

On the other side of the street a rustic café greets exhausted walkers and loud Jeep drivers.

100 m to the right of the café a path with steps leads upwards, past the deserted governor's residence (left), to the former Catholic chapel. Beyond that a rather dilapidated footpath runs up through the wildly romantic mountain landscape. Before the steps descend, you see a **vantage point** (745 m) on the right, where it is not difficult to find the right stone to take a rest on. The peak with the one antenna over on the side belongs to the military, the other one to the telephone companies. Spread out on the plain below is Apollónas. When visibility was good, the Italian governor de Vecci probably came up here, too, in order to reassure himself with his binoculars that his islands were still all there.

1.05

To descend, go down the steps, past the next peak, further downhill and, 30 m before the approach road to the antennas, left and below the old tennis court to the **hotels.**

1.25

Alternative: The path described below, hardly known any more even by the locals, is obliterated for a short stretch and hard to identify in some places. You must climb over harmless rocks a couple of times, but general orientation is not difficult. A few coloured markings help you along the way.

To avoid this, return down the same path you took on the way up.

1.25 Directly in front of the **hotels** a dirt road leads downhill between the ruins of the small barracks to the abandoned

1.30 **power plant**, now a store.

Beneath this is a spring called *Perivoli*. A monopáti begins at the well house and leads downhill immediately to the left of the metal water pipe. At first the path is clearly

1.35 recognisable, but ends at a moss-covered **stone house** (1.5 x 1.5 m). From here you walk without a path in the stream bed, then parallel with this on the left at a distance of 30 to 40 m. The water pipe is also on the right.

1.45 At a **scree slope** you leave the stream bed (**P2**: N36° 16.734'/E27°56.407'), climb up to the right to the water pipe and follow it into the valley. In doing so, you discov-

!! er the old descending path. In a flatter section, *on the right,* is a glade with low kermes oaks. (The pipe continues straight on down into a little forest.) You now go right and, behind the clearing, reach a path which traverses a gully (**P3**: N36°16.929'/ E27°56.573'). It brings you to the

2.10 **ascending** path, which you follow down left, down past

2.20 the shrine and left to the main street in **Sálakos**.

❷ A Wealth of Pictures in Fountouklí

The chapel of Áyios Nikoláos Fountouklí is one of the cultural highlights of Rhodes. This five-hour trek leads there from Sálakos, along partly very wide roadways which are easy to find and run through a shady forest and old olive groves.

■ *14 km, difference in altitude 120 m, difficult*

▷ *See map on previous page.*

AWT	Starting at the **Platía in Sálakos** (230 m), take the main
0.00	street for about 200m, ascending slightly, until you reach the Vrysakla fountain (right) and, diagonally opposite it, continue down a side street. With the cemetery 100 m to
0.05	the left, **past a concrete wall** on your left, you come to the shady valley ①. After the first stream bed, go right at the fork. In the next is a picnic spot (left) belonging to the local valley of the butterflies. Proceeding straight ahead, then uphill, you see Chálki and Alímia islands on the left.
0.10	At the **fork** you turn off right and, 100 m further on, left
0.15	at the water meter to reach the **Nicholas chapel** built in 2004. From there you continue down left to the upper edge of Pétala plain. Walking beneath pines, you enjoy a commanding view.
	After a shed (left) you pass through a gate, traverse more
0.30	ditches under giant oaks and arrive at a wide **glade with olive trees** (left). After another ditch you walk uphill to
0.40	the **dirt track** (P1: N36°17.046′/E27°57.953′, 250 m) and continue down to the left there.
	At a fork march uphill to the right, soon afterwards left

1.00	and cross a broad olive grove, at the end of which **goat pens** spread out. After this, the way continues down a
1.15	wide track, a firebreak. Go up right at the **turn-off** (P2: N36°16.668'/E27°59.191'). In a sparse olive garden you reach a tavern and then the ruins of an Italian manor.
1.40	Once on the road, go left to the **Áyios Nikoláos Fountouklí chapel** ② (P3: N36°16.460'/E27°59.844', 340 m), once part of a cloister.

> *This cross-in-square church with four apses or conchae was founded around 1500 by a high official in memory of his three children who had died of the plague. The family is depicted at eye level in the niche opposite the altar: the parents with the model of the church, the children praying in the Garden of Eden. Christ is blessing them. Next to him are his mother and John the Baptist.*
>
> *All the walls are completely covered with frescoes. Christ's baptism, Lazarus' resurrection and the Exodus from Egypt are depicted. Compassionately looking down at the weary wanderer from the dome are 25 saints.*

	You return the same way at first to the olive grove, but
1.45	there go down right on a roadway at the **second ruin**, walk between the trees on the level and later, at the sec-
1.50	ond **turn-off**, proceed left first downhill, then uphill. After the ascent you see the sea on both sides.
	On the ridge you first saunter along on flat terrain, see the Profítis Elías and then descend steeply to where the
2.05	**tracks cross** (P4: N36°16.955'/E27°52.439'). There you walk downhill to the left and after one minute turn off
!!	*sharply to the left!* The scents of the pines accompany you on your way down to the valley floor. The wide path
2.20	crosses the **stream bed** in a sharp left bend (P5: N36° 16.811'/ E27°59.108', 220 m). That is exactly where you follow the course of the stream 30 m downhill without a path, before going uphill to the left and, below a rock
2.25	(left), returning to the wide **sandy track** you took earlier. Now continue uphill to the right, past the goat pens and
2.45	down as far as the **fork** at a fence (P6: N36°16.972'/
2.55	E27°58.225'), where you go left to the **right turn-off**, via which you came up here (AWT 0.40). Now you walk up-
3.10	hill to the left, past a **sheep pen** (left) and later above the Nicholas Chapel to the festival ground with Christmas cave. After 100 m a dirt track leads down to the right to
3.25	**Sálakos**.

❸ The Castle on the Sea

*On this four-hour circular walking tour you pass
through a fertile valley on dirt roads, rest at a shady
village square, go for a swim in the sea and experience the sunset from the ruins of a crusader castle.
The shorter two-and-a-half-hour tour leaves out the
ascent to the village of Kritiniá.*

■ *11 km, difference in alt. 255 m, moderate to difficult*

AWT   The walk begins beneath the castle of Kritiniás (or Kástro
Kámeiros). If you come by **bus**, you must calculate an ad-
ditional two times 25 minutes/1.8 km to get there **from
Kámiros-Skála** on the road and back again. See map.

0.00   From the **lower car park** (with cantina, 95 m) of the
Kástro Kritiniás (p. 19) go back down the approach road
and turn right onto a narrow roadway after 80 m, later

0.05   turning left onto a wider **dirt road** and heading straight
on through a dip with a greenhouse (left). You can soon
see the goal up in the hills, the village of Kritiniá, and
above it the 1215 m high Atáviros, the loftiest peak on
Rhodes.

0.10   At a sharp **curve to the left** ① (**P1: N36°15.656'/
!!   E27°48.759'**) you turn down right onto a *5 m wide strip*
similar to a cultivated field. At the end of the strip bordered by low trees you can see a footpath leading downwards and accompanied by irrigation hoses. At the bot-

0.15   tom it meets a **roadway**, which you follow uphill left.

> *Short cut:* Later you will return to this place (= AWT
> 1.50/ **P2: N36°15.568'/E27°48.888'**). Now you could
> turn down right here and take the "**small tour**".

Turn left at the first fork, right at the following one and then, between greenhouses, along the foot of the slope rising to the left. Tomatoes, potatoes and many other vegetables are cultivated on this plain. At the **fork** go straight ahead. Above the path is a small **farmhouse**, surrounded by glorious chaos. 200 m beyond the house go uphill slightly to the left of the reeds and use a cement strip on the right to traverse the stream bed at the **crossing** in a small dip (**P3**: N36°15.354'/E27°49.540'). While working your way steeply uphill, enjoy the wonderful view of the castle and Chálki behind it.

0.20
0.30
0.35

0.40 Further up you come to a **water basin** (right). Continue on to the left. When the paths cross near a boulder (right), continue straight on uphill between olive trees. The path then continues in a wide arc to the right until the second

0.55 left turn at a **crossing.** Here you turn onto the *path dug into the ground* and leading uphill until you reach an old chapel.

*The white **Áyios Ioánnis Pródromos chapel** is located like a jewel, set between two cypress trees. Still preserved inside are soot-blackened, yet impressive frescoes from the time it was built, in the 13th or 14th century. The Sa-*

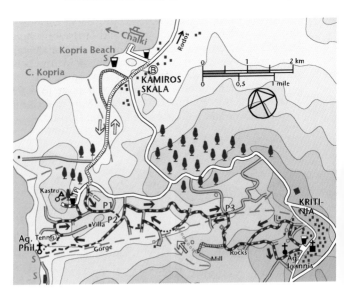

lome's Dance before Herod and the Beheading of John the Baptist are outstanding.

1.05 Following a cement path, we soon arrive at the shady village square, the "piatsa" of **Kritiniá** (255 m), for a well-earned rest.

After looking around this village, which was founded by the Cretans, and also having seen the remarkable church, we walk down the cement path along the left side of the piatsa facing the valley. Passing water basins (left), we continue straight on along a roadway and towards the valley in a wide arc to the left – disregarding a right turn-off. At times the path is almost flat and leads between the terraced fields, ending back at the crossing of the paths near the boulder, where we now wander downhill right to

1.25 the **water basin.**

> **Alternative:** If you turn left here, in a few minutes you will come to an oblong water basin from which a very old, round **grain mill** used to be operated.

1.30 The same path leads away from the water basin back down to the valley and turns to the left at the **reeds.** 80 m beyond the "chaos farmer's" walk down to the left. When

1.40 the dirt track ends, continue to the right towards a small house across a field to another **dirt track.** Follow it to the

1.45 right through green gardens and fields until it forks at a fence. Turning left, you come to an **equipment storage area**, after which you turn to the right at a small pump house. At the end of the dirt track a footpath connects to another dirt track, which you follow to the right. At the fork, head left 50 m in order to arrive back at the spot

1.50 where you **came downhill** earlier (=ATW 0.15, P2 see above).

This time you go downhill to the left into an intensively used fertile valley. The track ends to the right of a potato field. Of course, you discover the continuation of the

1.55 **path** immediately, as it leads on up to the right now. It meanders wonderfully above a rugged gorge ② and

2.15 through all the spices associated with Greek cuisine: thyme, sage, marjoram and many more. It ends at the **sea** in a flat coastal area where the ruins of the early Christian Philimon basilica ③ have been exposed. If you want to take a swim, there is a beach with sand further south.

Directly above the excavations a steep path marked by cairns leads to flat land with a country house (85 m), from

3   4

which you walk on to the left of the fence towards the
2.30   castle. Walk to the left on the **roadway**, leaving out two
left turns, continuing on beneath the castle ④, which pre-
sents itself from its wildly romantic side here. After passing it on the side, turn left at the crossing, continue uphill
along a road and you will arrive at the road leading to the
2.35   **castle.**

> *The **Kastro Kritinías** is the best preserved castle of the
> Order of St. John, erected on top of an older castle. The
> castle-keep, the gothic St. George's chapel and the shield
> wall are in good condition. The coats of arms of the
> Grand Masters of the Order, who had the castle con-
> structed beginning in 1472, are set in the outer walls.
> Their significance arose from their visual connection with
> the castle on the island of Alímia across the strait. The
> view across the sea to Chálki is especially enchanting to-
> wards evening.*

If you must return to **Kámiros-Skala** on foot, take the
way down to the parking area (along a small forest path)
and then along the road further downhill to the left. Perhaps you will still have the time and energy for a little visit to Johnny's lovely fish taverna at Kopriá Beach.

❹ Alpine Tour to Mount Atáviros

This six to seven-hour tour with a three-hour ascent through treeless fields ☐ should only be done by fairly experienced mountain hikers. But there are no dizzying heights. The way back calls for a sense of orientation. It is best to choose a fine day, as the danger of fog should not be underestimated. There are no cisterns.

■ *15 km, difference in altitude 780 m, difficult*

AWT	
0.00	On the left side of the street leading west in **Émbonas** (435 m) is a **wine tasting room** which you should rather pass by for the moment. After the curve take the first
0.04	**roadway** beyond the concrete wall, uphill to the left. This is where the *Villaré* grows, the best white wine on Rhodes.
0.15	The road narrows down to a **path** (P1: N36°13.201'/ E27°51.376', 536 m) which further up meets another roadway; walk along this on the level 30m to the right, then left up a path to another roadway, where you turn
0.20	off to the left. Below a **stone wall** (P2: N36°13.134'/ E27°51.458') ☐, turn left steeply uphill through boulders. There is a hut in the vineyard on the right. Shortly after this, climb over a fence using a ladder and walk along to
0.30	the right above the fence to another **ladder** and then from there continue laboriously uphill.
0.45	First to the left, then to the right of the scree chute as far as the topmost **small olive trees.** Then climb zigzag on
1.05	the left beside the chute – watch out for a **safety cable** which makes the going slightly easier. You will be glad to
1.30	finally reach the **edge of the cliff** at the top. Below the

	edge go right, later left, up between the rocks ③ until you
1.50	reach the **peak** with the fenced-off antenna installation
	(**P2**: N36° 12.554'/E27°51.812'). You have reached the
	highest point in the Dodecanese at 1215 m. Every few
	years there is even snow here. The new fence unfortunate-
	ly also surrounds the ruins of an old **temple to Zeus**. Be-
	hind the hills rotate the signs of the times.
1.55	On the right of the fence you descend to an old **footpath**,
2.10	which leads downhill in zigzag lines to the **road** and
	then, on the other side of the road but over to the side a
2.25	bit, out of the hollow and across the **road** again. The
	wonderful old mule track leads over the hill and gently
	downhill. Later, at a favourable spot, you drop down right
2.45	to the **dirt track.** After a few meanders above a gorge this
	brings you to a plateau further down, and you see the
3.00	**ruins of houses** (right) ④, (**P3**: N36°12.064'/E27°50.362',
	810 m); 100 m *in front of the electric cables.*

Alternative: The following description is of an old footpath which hardly anyone, even the locals, knows
about any more. Before you reach it, you have to work
your way through the phrýgana and the rocks without
a path for 25 minutes.

The alternative is to use the wide **dirt track** down to
the street (AWT 3.55), then to try and hitch a lift or

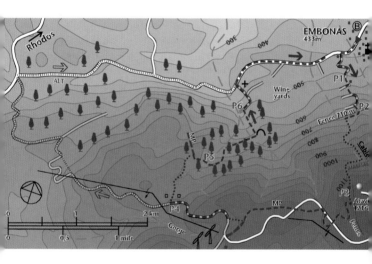

walk along the street for 4–5 km to reach Émbonas.

3.00	Having crossed the **ruins**, first walk in the ditch through the dip. Then continue about 30 m left of the ditch without a path and hop over the rocks. You now see Émbonas. Later the ditch is 100 m away to the right and covered with pines. You proceed almost on the level and come to a
3.30	light **pine forest.** There, go slightly down to the right – with a mountain ridge to your left – through the pines.
!!	Soon you cross an *indistinct path,* which takes you down
3.35	first to the right, then left and **crosses through the gorge** in a curve to the right (**P4:** N36°12.527'/E27°50.518').
★	The valley bed is to the left now, and a wildly romantic
!!	mountain path begins. It leads downhill at an *indistinct fork* and almost reaches the bottom of the gorge four minutes later. From here it continues almost on the level again across slabs of rock. Then it leads downhill, slightly to the left, towards a hollowed rock wall. In front of the
3.50	**caves,** shuffle downhill to the left. Where the two gorges
3.55	meet is a **watering place** for livestock (**P5:** N36°12.760'/E27°50.670'). There you pass through a gate, walk down-
4.00	hill to the left at the fork to the **road** and continue along it to the right. Maybe you can stop a helpful driver, for it
4.20	is still quite a way to **Émbonas.** Now at last the time has come to sample some *Villaré* in the wine-tasting room!

⑤ Mountain Meadows beneath Akramítis

A shady path leads up to the Akramítis massif and crosses through extensive, park-like mountain meadows. You can wander on past the chapel of St. John up to the peak. After a somewhat steep descent, you return to the road near Siána. The very beautiful tour lasts five hours, without any functioning cisterns. At several places you must pay careful attention to the turn-offs! If you have a hired care, drive as far as AWT 0.12

■ *9 km, difference in altitude 510 m, difficult*

AWT 0.00 0.12 !! !! 0.22	In **Monólithos** (310 m), at the **taverna** "Christos Corner", you walk up the street and 250 m after a right turn-off you notice a **parking area** to the right of the street. Across from it yellow cairns ☐ mark the way up the slope. In the woods turn *left* after 80 m at a cairn and then walk up the nice footpath. Another cairn later marks the **second turn-off** up to the right ② (**P1:** N36°08.215'/E27°44.454').
0.45 1.00 ★	The trek continues upwards, at first with some effort, but later very pleasantly between the pines, with a magnificent view of the broad Apolakkía Bay. At the **end of the ascent** (**P2:** N36°08.653'/E27°44.487', 610 m) wander down through the pine woods and uphill again, then on the level to the right of a ravine to a wonderful **glade** ③, where all the flowers of Greece bloom in spring, between age-old pines and cedars, ruins and decaying trees – a romantic painter like William Turner would probably have reached quickly for his sketch pad.

You ascend a few metres through violet sage blooms and cross over a stone wall which used to surround a field. From the other side of the wall it is only 200 paces until a phalanx of **cairns (P3: N36°09.201′/E27°45.020′)** direct the wanderer uphill *to the right* (and not straight on along the wider goat track).

1.10
!!

When you have passed above the cliff, gone left at the first **fork** at the top and again at the next one, another meadow stretches out in front of you, in which, to the left and barely perceptible, is the **chapel Áyios Ioánnis (P4: N36°09.247′/E27°45.252′)** The structure is plain except for the badly damaged frescoes in the old apse. Yet its situation in this abandoned area makes seeing it an experience.

1.15
1.25

Alternative: The rest of the way on down to Siána is uneven and bumpy. You might consider returning the

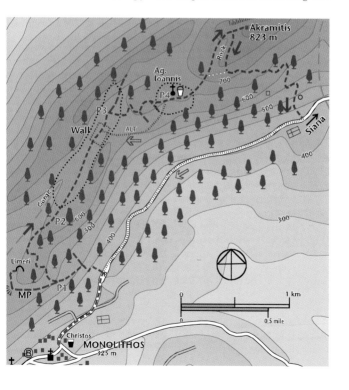

same way you came through the lovely meadows.

On the other side of the meadow a reddish-coloured path leads slowly up to an open meadow below a pine grove ④.

> *Short cut:* If you prefer not to climb right to the top, take the goat tracks on the right in the grove to traverse the rocky ridge, then turn left and follow the path which descends to Sianá.

Behind the pine grove a path leads down through a trough and then up again. At the last large tree, whose trunk branches at the top, you climb a few metres up through the rocks and reach a fork. (On the descent you return as far as this point.) Here you go left up to the fire

1.55 observation station and to the **summit of Akramítis** (823 m). The view over the dizzying cliffs over to Chálki is superb!

The way down into the valley first runs 200 m back to the

2.00 familiar **fork**, where it turns left. Then it proceeds horizontally to the left of the rocky ridge, before dropping towards the cairns and coloured dots. The pines and juniper bushes are only waist-high to begin with, but provide more shade further down between the rocks. The gravelly

2.30 track, though, becomes even steeper. After a round **lime**

2.40 **kiln** (left) you come to a 1.5m high **boulder** with a cairn.

2.45 Here you go left to the **road.**

(3.15) It is 30 minutes on foot down to **Monólithos**, hitch-hiking takes only 5 minutes.

It takes eight minutes uphill to reach **Siána**, with its narrow lanes and nice little tavernas. The village is famous for honey, yoghurt and especially *Zúmo*- a kind of grappa.

⑥ Monólithos

On this wonderful six-hour tour you circle at a respectful distance round the crusader castle enthroned on a steep cliff. There are several possibilities for taking a swim and then a terrific sunset at the end. The route may be shortened.
■ *13 km, difference in altitude 315 m, difficult*

AWT
0.00

From the old **village fountain** in **Monólithos** (315 m) you saunter uphill at the plane tree, after a right-hand bend you go downhill along the street above the gardens on the right and turn to the right at the last houses ① onto a cement path which is soon flanked on the left with walls of loess. It leads through terraces of olive trees straight down to the valley floor. There you turn right onto a **roadway** and proceed straight along it after the dip.

0.10

0.15
!!

At the fork, go to the left - don't miss the **dirt road** leading *downhill to the left* after a small olive grove.

At the end of the road, walk to the right past the grapevines and then take a half-right between two cornfields to the right edge of the forest, where you unknot and refasten a **gate** (**P1:** N36°07.180'/E27°44.357'). You will find a sufficient number of red dots in the sparse pine forest to soon reach the next **edge of the forest.** Charred tree trunks from the fire in 1999 later stand in front of the sea like skeletons. Take the bright rocky peninsula on the right of the broad mountain ridge ② as your goal. The **rocky Foúrni Cape** lies on the right at the end of the way.

0.20

0.25

1.00

There are several early Christian caves in the peninsula's steep east sandstone coast. Some of these are said to be

over 1000 years old. Beneath the stony remains of the medieval watchtower on the point is a cruciform cave church in which a grave was found.

1.05 The wide pebble beach boasts a **cantina.** (Behind the parking starts a dirt track up to the village). From there the asphalt road runs between pines to a beautiful and
1.15 empty **beach.** Better make the most of this, for now the way becomes strenuous as you climb 115 metres altitude up the road. On the hill, to the left of the road, is a rock formation in the shape of a dragon, like the one slain by St. George (**P2:** N36°06.924'/E27°43.090'). It marks the
1.45 **sandy path** leading downhill to the left behind it.

Short cut: Take the road to Monólithos for an hour.

Continue along the sandy path to the left, from which a turn-off leads down to the left. Our path straight ahead offers beautiful views of Cape Armenistís and the island of Chálki as you walk downhill. After a curve to the right you can look up to Mount Akramítis, to the small white chapel halfway up and to the monolith with the fortress, whose walls seem to grow out of the cliff. The path starts
2.10 to climb again. 80 m after a **vineyard** (right) you can begin looking for the way further up ③, but first wander on
2.20 to the chapel of **Áyios Georgios.**

On the right inside the simple chapel rides the dragon-killer. In front there is a shady spot for a picnic, with a

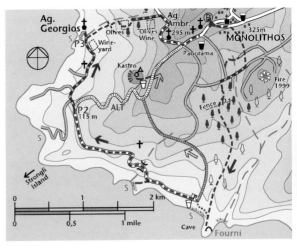

bell made from a grenade shell – divine. Down below by the water, a mini-bay!

On the way back you must be very careful not to miss the
2.25 **turn-off** 3 *to the left* with the *cairns,* which comes 4 to 5
!! minutes later (**P3:** N36°07.657'/E27°43.152'). An old, somewhat decayed path leads uphill along a stream bed, turns onto a roadway on the right after 8 minutes, continues upwards, crosses a dilapidated fence twice and ends at
2.35 the beginning of a **roadway.** This leads along flat ground
2.50 to the left and then up through pines to a **glade** with olives and grapevines. From there continue on uphill to
2.55 the right to a wide, level **road** and then to the right again,
3.05 past the **Ambrosius Chapel** (295 m) to the fork in the road.

*The romantically inclined now walk downhill to the right for 12 minutes to the **Kástro Monólithos** 4 and enjoy the famous **panorama at sunset.***

Always a fortified place of asylum, an important castle of the Order of St. John stood here from 1476. Only ruins still remain. The chapel of St. Panteléimon was added on later. Then, as now, the view over to the neighbouring islands is stupendous.

The others can turn off to the left to end a day's walking
3.20 in the taverna **"Panorama".** Not bad either way!

❼ Asklipío

*Untouched by tourism, the village of Asklipío offers
an absolute gem: the wonderful frescoes in the
church. The three to four-hour walk along dirt roads
offers panoramic sea views on the way back and
ends at a lovely sandy beach. You must get off the
bus, or leave your hired car, just before Gennádi!*

■ *11 km, difference in alt. 180 m, easy to moderate*

AWT	Beyond the beach hotels of Kiotári is a petrol station on the right-hand side of the coast road. 300 m later is a bridge, and after another 300 m you must ask the bus dri-
0.00	ver to stop opposite the "Villa Maria". A **sandy path** leads next to a pump house (left) into the island's interior. You pass a yard for building materials, keep to the right at one fork and turn left at the next. Then the path continues slightly uphill, with the massive concrete wall of a gravel-
0.15	pit on the right. At the **fork** beyond it, turn to the right onto the Katáchra river plain. Up on the right lies Asklipío
0.40	village with castle. The right-angled **turn-off to the right** (**P1:** N36°14.276'/E28°09.317') brings you through the dry stream bed, then to the left and later uphill. Amble
0.50	along below the St. George's chapel and past a **well** and soon, after a curve, you are greeted by the sprawling white village ①. Below the village you cross the asphalt road and
1.00	walk uphill along the narrow, twisting lanes to **Asklipío.** Proceeding beneath the belltower, you come to the famous church of **Kímissi tis Theotókou.**

*The church is dedicated to Mary's Passing Away. The
original chapel from 1060 had the shape of a Latin cross*

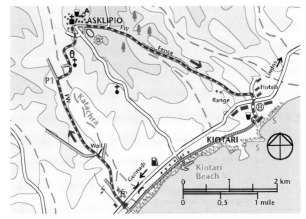

and was later expanded with side aisles and painted in the 17th century. In the nave you can see the genesis, the creation of the world, in the right transept the Revelation of St. John, in the left one frescoes from the life of Christ.

1.10 After that you first walk along the lane to the right of the cafe "Platía" and soon find the way up to the **castle ruins** ②. Only a few remains are to be seen from the time of the Hospitallers, but the beautiful view more than makes amends.

To descend, aim for the sports field, which you can reach without a path between olive trees. The sandy field should stay to your right below the road. After 100 m, at
1.20 the next **turn-off**, go down the roadway on the right and always stay on the wider path through the sparse pine forest at the subsequent turn-offs. The fence on the left
1.45 serves to keep wild goats out. The **clay pigeon shooting**
2.05 **range** remains to the right before you take a **street** downhill to the right to the hotel "Rodos Maris" and arrive at
2.10 the **bus station.**

Circular tour: To get back to your car, take the road along the beach.

⑧ Moní Thári – saved from the flames

"Anyone who wants to wander through a Greek forest at some time …" is how this description used to commence. In July 2008 this forest was ravaged by a fire. Yet because the region has plenty of water, it should recover soon. Already six weeks after the fire it was possible to discern the first signs of vegetation – we will be watching it closely!

In four hours the route leads along tracks, which aren't too steep, to the famous St. Michael's cloister in Thári and then returns to Laérma in a wide curve. You will only find a well in Thári.

It is best to reach the starting point Laérma with a hired car or by taxi from Lárdos.

■ *12 km, difference in altitude 100 m, moderate*

AWT 0.00	After **Laérma Church** (right/285 m) you pass by the inn "Igkos" (left) on the slightly ascending street. The innkeeper Panagiotis willingly tells hikers more about the fire. 200m beyond the well (right) you leave the street after a right bend, dropping left onto an initially asphalt track. On the left stand the first charred trees. The other side of the valley was spared ①.
0.11 0.25 0.30	At the **fork** continue straight on downhill, going right further down and right again at the next **fork** (P1: N36°08.513'/E27°55.704'). Soon after you come past a military depot (right). Where the path forks, bear left downhill, then directly afterwards right and through a **stream bed.**
	At the following crossroads you go on uphill and then

0.55   through scorched hilly country to **Thári Cloister** ☒ (P2: N36°07.987′/E27°54.996′). It was specially protected during the forest fire.

> *The cloister, dedicated to the archangel Michael, accommodates 15–20 monks. It also sends forth missionaries. Visitors can view the old, completely painted church, whose oldest, 600-year-old frescoes are in the chancel. Saint Michael can be seen several times, with his sword in the right hand and a child in the left. He is fighting against the powers of darkness with his sword and accompanying mankind's soul, symbolically represented by*

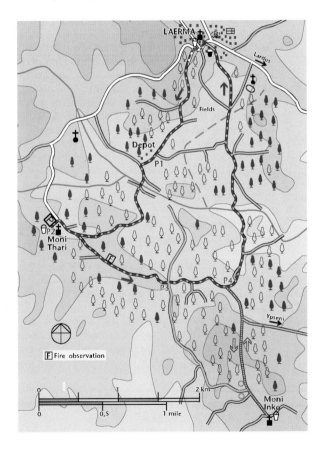

*the child, into eternity. A particular feature is a represen-
tation of a seated Christ.*

To continue, walk back a short distance and uphill to the
right at the fork above the cloister. On the left of the ridge
is Mt. Atáviros, the highest peak on Rhodes (1215 m) .
At the foot of this mountain started the fire which, in one
week, ate its way right through the island as far as Lárdos
– all because of the carelessness of a farmer. Burning animals and exploding pine cones fed the flames.

1.05	Soon you reach the fire **observation station** along the way. Already in 1987 and 1992 there were devastating fo-
1.20	rest fires. At the **crossing of the paths** (**P3:** N36° 07.781'/E27°55.883') you proceed straight ahead. Disre-
1.25	gard a **right turn-off**, but after ascending to 285 m take
1.45	the **left turn-off** into the valley (**P4:** N36°07.477'/ E27°56.508'). The fire raged most here. But just six weeks later the first green was noticeable again .

Alternative: Straight on to Inko Cloister in 1/4 hour.

1.45	After the left turn-off you come to a wide forest track run- ning downhill, ignore a wide right turn and descend into the valley, where the village of Laérma comes into view again up above.
2.00	After the **dry stream bed** (190 m) you ascend through al-
2.25	most unscorched earth and, at a forked **crossroads** resem- bling a three-pronged pitchfork, walk up through the
2.35	middle to **Laérma**.

⑨ The Acropolis of Líndos

Except by taking a boat, this trek is surely the loveliest way to get to Líndos. Walking for three hours along well-marked goat tracks amidst olive trees and oaks, one traverses a dramatic rocky valley and proceeds along a marvellous mountain ridge, but without any watering-places. It is possible to return to Rhodes by boat.

■ *11 km, difference in alt. 185 m, easy to moderate*

AWT
0.00 — The **bus stop of Vlichá** (50 m) lies behind the major crossroads. From there it is about 200 m along the road to Líndos to two bridges, but before them you turn off to the right onto a dirt road and immediately left into a dry stream bed. On the other side, continue uphill more or less to the right towards the rock face, without a path through

0.10 — olive terraces. To the right of the **corner of a fence** (**P1:** N36°06.392′/E28°03.494′) you still bear right across a dry

0.15 — bed until you come to a **roadway**, where you go right

0.20 — and, at the next fork, left. After a **gate** the track brings you into an impressive gorge ① lined with pines.

Before the roadway later leads to the right through the

0.30 — dry bed, proceed straight ahead along a **path** marked by cairns – leaving the dry bed and the roadway on the right. The path enters a wide hollow in which an olive grove comes into view on the left and a cave straight ahead on the

0.40 — slope. This **cave** (**P2:** N36°05.690′/E28°03.215′) should be entered cautiously, as it is where the sheep take their siesta. Besides, as every classics scholar knows, Greek caves tend to be inhabited by a Cyclops.

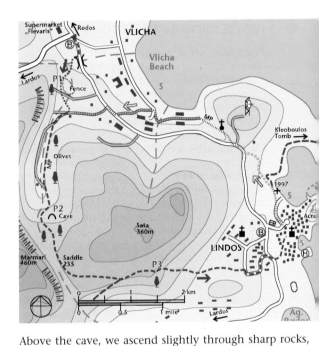

Above the cave, we ascend slightly through sharp rocks, between which inquisitive "stone men", or cairns, look out curiously ☑. Kermes oaks provide shade for the path, which meanders – somewhat to the right – along the foot

0.55 of Mt. Marmári. Having reached the **saddle** (235 m), we go downhill. At the end of the plateau which follows we can see the sea again. Further down our route runs to the left along a hardly visible path which is accompanied on the right by a dry wall. The lovely view across the sea and up to a chapel on a peak should not divert our attention

1.25 away from the cairns! They lead us to an **elevation** (P3: N36°05.216'/E28°04.111'), from which the ancient acropolis of Líndos comes into view. The cluster of little old houses is still hidden in the hollow.

The rest can be told quickly. Disregarding the new buil-

1.55 dings on the plateau, you just look forward to **Líndos**.

Circular tour: If you've left a car in Vlichá, follow the alternative route shown on the map.

⑩ Two Castles

During this five to six-hour walk along the coastline you have a chance to visit the ruins of two medieval castles. In between you have magnificent coastal scenery and several sandy beaches. The length of the well-marked trail calls for stamina, but it can be shortened. A well offers refreshment. Find out bus departure times from Charáki in advance!

■ *12 km, difference in alt. 205 m, moderate to difficult*

AWT   The **castle of the Order of St. John** (15th century) in the rural town of **Archángelos** is our point of departure. Very little remains to be seen inside the restored bulwark. Like Féraklos, it mainly served as a refuge for the population. Beneath the castle, walk along the castle away from the

0.00 **steps** towards the table-top mountain without a path, with the town on the right. On the ridge, look for a way

0.05 left through the rocks, descend as far as the **field track** on the right of the olive grove ①, go left until you reach a

0.10 wider **sandy track**, which you take left again through the groves.

> *Short cut:* By heading to the right across the ridge and then right, you save 1½ hours.

0.15 Three minutes later, after passing a solitary **boulder** (right), change direction at a sharp corner to the right and walk through the pleasant farming countryside towards

0.25 the sea. At the **fork** go straight ahead and, after 120 m,

!!   *right at the cairns* onto a narrow footpath between the rocks (**P1:** N36°12.527'/E28°07.750'). Later you see the holiday village of Stégna, which has developed a lot re-

cently – as audibly demonstrated by the cheers of the animators there.

0.40   The path leads down between the rocks in an arc **above Stégna.** We wander south through the olive groves on the plateau, to the left of two lumps of rock ②. A dirt track to the right of the fences brings us to a scree path, which as-

1.00   cends steeply up to a **ridge** (100 m).

From there, you proceed left along the wider dirt road and go right at a fork. Further along the dusty track you encounter a well – a rarity in this region, which is now badly scarred by the ravages of development. Then you go left

1.20   and arrive at the **Bay of Klisoúras.**

After a swim, take the track heading west behind the fenced-off houses, climb up to the chapel without a path and thence inland to the roadway. Soon you reach a long

1.35   rectangle cut into the rocks: an **ancient quarry**, as you can still tell from the steps. The stones for Líndos, opposite, were probably hewn here.

On the opposite narrow side of the rectangle a red dot di-

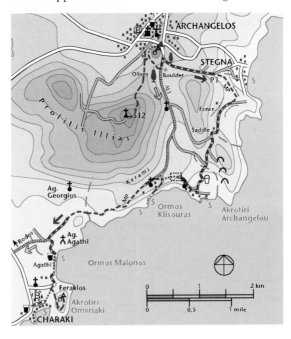

rects you right, into a bizarre rocky landscape ③. Cross
1.45 the **dirt road** which you later encounter by going up to
the left.

> *Alternative:* If you go left down the track as far as a soli-
> tary bare olive tree, you find a path running down to
> the perfect beach beneath the cliffs called Kokkini
> Ammos.

1.50 Three **little houses** and a chapel stand alone on the
plateau. On the inland side of the houses a roadway con-
1.55 tinues across the plateau and at the **end** of it is a path. You
can avoid a rather steep area by going above it to the
right. Then the landscape plays another trump. If you
look back, you see a gigantic rock gate which makes you
★ think of Salvadore Dalí ④. Before the field head left towards the hill. To the right you can see the St. George's
2.25 chapel. The wanderer is penned in by a **double fence** and
then continues along a dirt track around a stone hill. Later it would be possible to turn off to the right at a wide
fork and reach the main road sooner. Otherwise you come
2.40 to the **sandy bay of Agáthi** with its lively beach, inns
and chapel (found it?). The bay is surrounded by the ruins
of the castle and unfinished structures. On the dirt track
2.50 you pass the **sign** to the castle.

> The huge, now empty **Féraklos Castle** was torn away
> from Byzantium by the Order of St. John in 1306 and
> was its first castle on Rhodes. Not until 1523, i.e. after
> the town, did it become Turkish.

If the ascent is too steep, it is easy to walk through the
2.55 meadows to **Charáki**.

⓫ The Cloister of Tsambíka

This cloister, situated on a lofty peak, is the destination for today's five-hour trek. The ascent is from the most beautiful beach on Rhodes, up through rocky terrain. Refreshments can be found at the beach as well as near the cloister.
The starting point is Archángelos, which can easily be reached by bus. By alighting earlier, it is possible to tramp to the beach and thus take a short cut.
■ *8 km, difference in alt. 340 m, moderate to difficult*

AWT

0.00 Starting at the middle bus stop in **Archángelos** (with a bust/ 150 m), you walk back as far as the cemented stream bed on whose northern side is a **small WC**. From there, leave the main street to the right by taking the street on the left of the dry bed. After three minutes go straight ahead. Walk 100 m directly along the stream and then up

0.05 the **roadway** to the left until you come 50 m below dirty pens.

0.10 Here you veer **left** and, 20 m further on, right and cross a hollow with olive trees. To the left of the fence on the next hill you find a field track going left. At the next fork in the little forest, bear right and, past a rather chaotic looking farm pen, continue uphill to the road.

Go 300m downhill to the right along this road and then

0.25 uphill to the left at a small **private chapel** (P1: N36° 13.077'/E28°07.823'). You catch sight of today's destination up on the mountain: the cloister of Tsambíka ⓵. Behind the concrete wall of a villa (right), descend right and after 20 m, below a fence, left. After about 200 m you pass

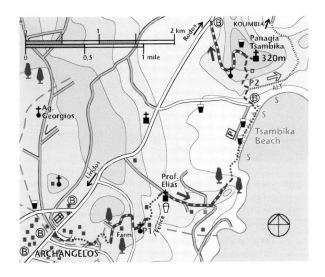

a gate and a few tethered dogs. Then a narrow path runs in a right-hand arc between pines to the roadway at the

0.40 small **Profítis Elias Cloister**, sited in a garden. The key hangs on the left, should you wish to draw water.

Beside the wall of the cloister, go down the field track, tur-

0.50 ning left at the fork. At the **left turn-off** further down you proceed a short distance straight ahead through the

!! olive grove, but turn off *to the left 15 m before the rocks* on the left side.

Your way continues along a rough dirt track *directly on the right of the olive grove* – not in the phrýgana. From the lo-wer edge of the grove a new roadway leads right, through a sparse pine forest ② to a slope with fine sand ③. Swing

1.05 downhill in elegant slalom curves to the **sandy beach of Tsambíka.** Empty the sand out of your shoes, change your clothes, take a break!

After that you stroll over to the far end of the beach (with the quieter places for a swim) and, on the left beside the

1.15 **bus station kiosk**, look for the water pipes which run along the ground diagonally uphill to the left ④. Follow them a few metres, then, before the pens, turn upwards to the right at a right angle. Cairns already await you! To the left of your steep path stands an outcrop of rock. Where

1.25	you reach the same level as it (80 m), the path **forks** (P2: N36°13.945'/E28°08.930').

One could hike to Kolímbra on the right. But we head left, almost on the level. Then turn steeply uphill to the right again, with a steep outcrop on the left. Climb uphill in wide curves to a spot where you have to cross over an outcrop on the left. If you have a great fear of heights, you must keep looking towards the right for five metres. As a reward, you reach a magnificent picnic spot right away. Down below is the beach and its little restaurants, which have staked out their claims.

1.50	Through a sparse pine forest you come to **ruins** (right)
1.55	and steps leading uphill to the **car park.** You share the last 297 steps with panting motorists until you arrive at
2.05	the **cloister of Tsambíka**, or Our Dearly Beloved Virgin.

The guest is received in the courtyard. There are some dormitories for women who wish to bear children: a night on the mountain is said to have helped produce offspring even in difficult cases. That's why a lot of photographs of healthy infants can be seen on the chapel's left wall. St. Charámbolos looks positively old in comparison.

The descent down the steps leads to a restaurant with a terrace, where you can sit as if you were on a quiet Alpine meadow and look down upon the huge hotels in Kolímbia. You can smile hopefully at a car driver here or else walk down the road for 15 minutes and hop onto the next

2.30	bus in the **main street.**

⑫ A Thrill at the Eptá Pigés

The seven-hour circular tour leads along dirt tracks through countless olive groves to the Eptá Pigés (seven springs) with garden restaurant and then on to some orange gardens. The shortened tour lasts five to six hours.

■ *15 km, difference in alt. 85 m, moderate to difficult*

AWT	
0.00	About 20 metres north of the cement stream bed at the central bus stop in **Archángelos** – opposite the **police station** –, enter the "Odos Stadioy", go right at the next
0.07	fork, then straight on and across the **by-pass road.**
0.15	Follow an alley and turn left at a pointed **garden wall.** Shortly afterwards you see the St. George's chapel in the olive groves on the left.
0.20	300 m further, at the **fork,** go left uphill beneath pines
0.30	and later beneath a **power line.** At the right turn-off in front of a fence, proceed straight on and then downhill onto a broad plain five minutes later. 300 m beyond the
0.45	**Stilianos chapel** (right) you take the *second,* right-angled
!!	**turn-off** to the right into the valley (**P1:** N36°14.924'/
0.50	E28°06.764'), where you veer left.
	Along a dirt track you reach a little street and walk downhill to the right to a round "well". If you look into it, you will hear a bubbling noise – and voices. It is the ventilation shaft for the water tunnel. From there you first walk
1.05	left over the hill to the **Eptá Pigés,** which lie behind the shady garden restaurant.

Downstream from the springs is the beginning of a narrow tunnel ① which transports the water through the

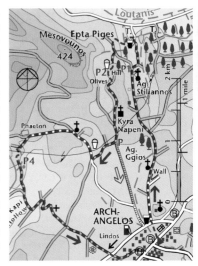

mountain. Passing through the narrow shaft affords a real thrill. If you find it too narrow, walking back over the two hills will also bring you to the small, romantic reservoir. Below this is a further tunnel. The system was installed by the Italians to supply water to Kolímbia.

1.05 Behind the **bridge in the garden restaurant** you follow the footpath to the left. Then proceed steeply uphill to

1.10 the right in the thick pine forest in order to reach an **olive terrace**, which you traverse through the middle. At the end of this grove, walk left uphill without a path to another olive grove, go left there and continue with the fence on your left.

Later you cross through the grove to the right without a path and come to a dirt track, which you follow to the left. After three minutes you bear right in front of a fence and head directly for a wide hill. (Straight ahead leads to the Stilianos chapel you passed on the way up.)

1.25 Before reaching the hill, you go right, past a **well** (left), making a left curve round the hill. After three minutes

!! you discover *two 1.5 m high boulders* (**P2:** N36°14.892'/ E28°06.526') *and 40 m beyond them* a path leading uphill ②. At the top you follow a dirt track to the right as far as

1.45 the small **Kyra Napeni monastery** ③.

From here you continue straight on, past the turn-off (to the right), and down across expansive olive groves. Shortly after passing beneath the power line, leave the path

1.55 you have been using at the **turn-off** in front of a fence to the right (**P3:** N36°14.072'/E28°06.620').

Short cut: If you proceed straight ahead, you reach

the village of **Archángelos** in about 35 minutes.

Walking under olive trees, you later descend left at a fork beneath the power line, alongside water channels and

2.05 then reach a **road**. Here you go right and, beside the tiny chapel, left as far as a walled-in enclosure where wild

2.20 ponies are bred. It is called "**Phaethon**" after Alexander the Great's horse.

To the left of the wall you follow the dirt track. At a fork you go down to the left and, after 300 m, beyond a ditch, drop left onto a footpath ④. In front of a fence you swing right and, beyond a small waterfall, follow the tracks leading left into the tropical valley. Next to irrigation channels you come to a roadway. You are now in the **Kápi valley** which, with plenty of water, boasts many orange gardens. Half way up the hillside are two concealed stalactite caverns.

2.40 Following the roadway, you pass a small **pond** (left) (**P4:**

2.50 N36°14.001'/E28°05.528', 125 m). Ignore a **right turn-off**, turning off left up the hill at a T-junction after three minutes. After another three minutes the way ascends steeply to the right at a crossing.

3.00 **At the top** you proceed straight ahead on the same level past two crossroads and across the by-pass road to arrive

3.35 in **Archángelos**.

⑬ The Hot Springs of Kalithéa

The easy three to four-hour walk along roadways offers sweeping views across the island. Awaiting walkers are the hot springs of Kalithéa beside the sea and bizarre rocky bays with nice beach restaurants.
■ *6 km, difference in altitude 120 m, easy*

AWT

0.00

!!

0.06

0.15

In the preserved village of **Koskinoú** take the lane on the left of the mini-market opposite the fountain on the rather oversized **main square** and keep walking in this direction until you come to a transverse street, which you walk up to the right for 150 m. Disregard the "Odos Ag. Eirínis", instead turning left into the side street *20 m further on,* in which you soon see a small chapel. Gradually ascending to the **by-pass road**, you see a bus stop on the left and beyond it the rocky "mountain" – but more of that later.

At the fork that soon follows you turn left, continue climbing slowly until you reach the plateau, where you walk straight ahead and, at a **group of houses**, left. Where there is an incline beside a villa in a stone garden, the "mountain" turns out to be a hollow tooth. It is a quarry.

Descending again, you have an impressive view of the beach hotels in Faliráki. In the tight right-hand bend (**P1:** N36°22.801'/E28°13.537', 120 m) you leave the road by proceeding straight on into a dirt track. After 80 m you bear right, towards the chapel and the antennas. This is where a residential quarter is being built overlooking our destination: the hot springs of Kalithéa, down to the right

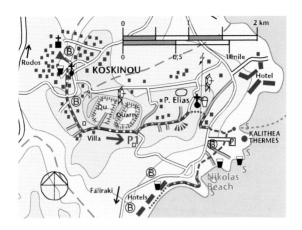

by the sea. To the north the city of Rhodes soon comes in-
0.35 to view as well. Then you arrive at the **chapel of Profitis
Elías** with its beautiful icons, a well and a panorama view.
Descend the slope of the cliff without a path, 80 m to the
right of the antenna, and look for a dirt track leading
0.45 down to the **main road** and then, on the opposite side,
0.55 paths running down to the **hot springs of Kalithéa.**

*In 1929 the Italians built the oriental-style thermal
baths. The "red water" from the rock source, renowned
since Antiquity, is said to heal almost any ailment. At
that time it was an attraction for international society,
but the buildings later fell into disrepair. In 2007, loving-
ly restored, they were reopened. For a small admission
charge it is possible to visit the usually sheltered, but
sometimes quite busy bathing bay. The pump room is a
must, though ①, and the view out to sea! There is a bus
stop on the road.*

Let yourself drift southwards along the rocky coast under
1.20 the pines. Two **rocky bays** with shady beach taverns
await you ②! If you prefer sand, try the long beautiful
1.30 **strand of Faliráki.**

Κάρπαθος
Kárpathos

The mountainous island of Kárpathos is the second largest of the Dodecanese. At the narrowest point the island is only four kilometres wide, but it is ten times as long. Together with its sister islands Kássos and Saría, it rises up on a broad undersea base which stretches from the Greek mainland to Turkey. The sea falls away to a depth of 2500 metres on both sides of the archipelago. Tourism has been established to a limited extent in the flat southern section. Although tourism is an important source of income, it does not dominate everything. Road construction has thus been carried out with a certain sense of proportion, so many old mule tracks can still be found. The hiker is more attracted to the middle of the island and to its northern part. These regions rank among the most beautiful hiking areas in the Aegean. You can walk through shady pine forests, olive groves and magnificent rocky landscapes along old pack-mule tracks to get to chapels and villages which have only recently been supplied with electricity. And where, for example in picturesque Ólympos, centuries-old traditions and customs are preserved. Here you can occasionally listen to music played on archaic instruments like the lyre and lute and accompanied by spontaneous singing as you try the island's excellent specialities.

Recently hiking trails have been cleaned and marked. In some regions the traces of forest fires in 1990 and 2004 can still be found.

Particularly beautiful hikes are those described in numbers 20, 21, 22, 23 and 24. Tours 18 and 22 can also be done on a boat excursion to Diafáni.

⑭ Along Old Paths to Lefkós

Along old mule paths it takes four to five hours to wander down to the beautiful beaches of Lefkós via Mesochóri. In 2004 a fire destroyed parts of the previous pine forest, but it is slowly growing again. Tavernas are to be found in Mesochóri and Lefkós, and a well along the route.

It is possible to drive to the windmills in the saddle before Spóa by taxi or bus. After Lefkós there are no taxis, but in high season a bus.

■ *13 km, difference in alt. 390 m, moderate to difficult*

AWT	At the fourth **windmill** ① (390 m) from the left a trekking
0.00	path (KA 18) drops down to a **country lane.** Here you go
0.03	right for a short while and left at the first roadway. It leads to the chapel Agíi Anárgiri dedicated to the saints Kosmas and Damian and further on round a narrow valley as far
0.20	as a massive **paled gate.** In front of it you go left and across the meadow. Behind a house you find a footpath, which soon affords wonderful sea views through pines ②. Then you proceed almost on the same level across ter-
0.35	races, which later offer a **view** of a chapel down below. From here the path is lined with dense vegetation. After
0.45	the **Saint Charálambos chapel** ③ (P1: N35°38.128′/ E27°07.197′; 160 m) you cross a modest ridge with vine-
1.00	yards and come to **Mesochóri.** Below the Panagía church it is possible to drink water from a spring or even something more substantial at Stéki, view of the village inclusive.
1.10	We leave the village at the bottom near a tiled **chapel** ④,

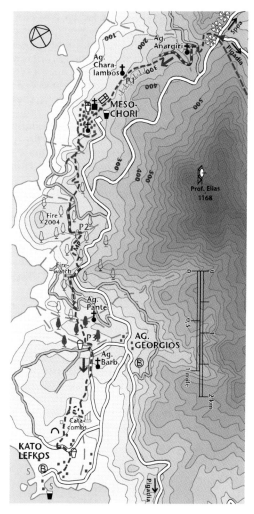

below which a concrete footpath commences on the right. At the turn-off shortly afterwards we go right and, at the next **fork**, left.

1.13

Moving along between old dry-stone walls, which protect olive groves and gardens, you turn right downhill at another **fork** and then traverse a flat ridge. The hiker is re-

1.17

★ warded with a picture-book landscape criss-crossed by
1.30 old, well preserved paths ⑤. After a trough a steep **set of steps** winds its way up the rocky flank of the mountain to a ridge, offering a final view of Mesochóri. Here you see the first traces of the fire in 2004.

On the far side of the ridge you cross a roadway and on the other side, slightly above you, you notice tree skele-
1.40 tons. A **roadway** alongside a power line runs over a plateau, exactly 1000 m below the peak of Profitis Elias rising up on the left (1168 m). At the end of the roadway you descend into a **valley formed by erosion (P2: N35°**
1.50 **36.976'/ E27°05.733')** and, on the other side, climb up a wide, paved kalderími for some time ⑥ until reaching the
2.10 **road.** Walk right along it, right again at the fire observation tower and, after 15 m, left down to a roadway.
2.15 From there metal signs show us the **way right**, down to the old paved path, which soon crosses a roadway. On the far side, displaced diagonally to the left, you find mark-ings on a narrow path to the left of a new olive grove. 150 m to the left you see the Panteleimon Chapel. The
2.40 path now meanders through unburnt terrain and a **small ravine (P3: N35°36.028'/ E27°05.340').**
2.45 After the short ascent you come across a **well** on the right and immediately after it a little asphalt road, where you proceed straight ahead along it. On the left are the **Barbara Chapel** and the dwellings of the scattered settle-ment Áyios Geórgios in the fields. 200 m beyond the chapel you follow the signs to the cistern on the right. At the end of the lane, in front of the garden encircled by
2.55 stones, a few paces will bring you to the **Roman cisterns** on the left.

It is still in dispute whether these are cisterns or cata-combs. It is only certain that the underground room, which is supported by 15 pillars, dates back to Roman times.

From here, return 50 m the way you came. Before the ruins of some houses, turn left onto a trekking path and then later left again onto a wider path which leads across
3.05 barren, stony moorland to a small hill. After the **water tank** (right), a monopáti begins to lead downhill. After a few metres you can see the cave on the right.

As shown by the remains of shells on the ceiling, it was most probably once under the sea, then pushed upwards and has been used by mankind from time immemorial. Wall niches on the sides could have been graves. The walls, which were later added to create animal pens, make this an extremely picturesque place.

From the cave, continue downhill, going left at the water tank, then right at the next crossing and arriving down at
3.15 one of the **beaches in Lefkós.** And now just jump into the water.

In early Christian times a city with 30,000 inhabitants used to stand here. It was protected by the fortress Sókas-tro on the island just off the coast. Remains of buildings there also bear testimony to fortifications from Byzantine and Venetian times.

▶ The car rental firm in Lefkós can help you to get back.

⑮ Kalí Límni, the Beautiful Lake

No one knows where this name for a mountain comes from. "Kalí", or "beautiful", is certainly the right word though. This eight-hour trek is strenuous yet unforgettable. Besides long, almost flat stretches it features the steep climb up to Kalí Límni, at 1215 m the second highest mountain in the Dodecanese – after Atáviros on Rhodes. The hiker sees the variety of landscapes on Kárpathos: its charming west side and the magnificently wild east coast.

However, on days with heavy cloud cover there is the danger of losing orientation on the mountain. While perseverance is required, a head for heights is not. Water can be found at several places, and even a taverna at the foot of the mountain. An insider's tip: take along swimming things.

The tour can be shortened by taking a taxi to Lástos.

■ *20 km, difference in altitude 925 m, difficult*

AWT Take the bus to Voláda or have the driver drop you off two minutes later at the turn-off to "Kalí Límmi" (see ALT on the map).

0.00 In **Voláda** (470 m), walk uphill at the apartment building ①, but then leave the steep alley lined with walls three minutes later to turn left onto a footpath. Shortly after-

0.05 wards, turn right onto a **roadway**, which ends unexpectedly in a field. At the other end on the right you reach a somewhat overgrown monopáti which, later becoming a roadway, leads to a concrete track, which you take steeply

0.12 up to the left as far as the road. At the **fountain** from the

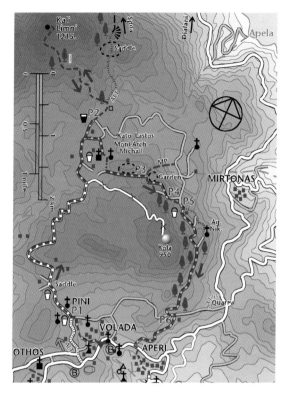

year 2000 (**P1**: N35°33.138'/ E27°09.226') you take a right turn and continue uphill, above the lovely high valley with the scattered houses of the hamlet Píni.

0.25 The little road crosses a **saddle**, where you can enjoy not only fresh well water but also a wonderful view of the charming west coast all the way to Kássos. The occasionally breathtaking vistas make you forget the asphalt. Gradually today's destination, Kalí Límni, comes into view, with the **Lástos plateau** ☑ beneath it to the right.

1.10 At the **fork**, the asphalt road leads up to the right to a military installation, but you should walk left along the sand

1.15 to the houses on the **Lástos plateau** (725 m). Where this ends, you can get the inn-keeper Thanássis to reserve a

1.25 place for later in the **taverna** (**P2**: N35°34.781'/ E27°08.368').

Take leave of the fertile gardens and fields at the roadway between the taverna and the farmhouse and, 100 m later,

1.30 turn left onto a trekking path leading to a **solitary tree** ③.

Alternative: On days when visibility is only mediocre, you are well advised to forego the peak and choose the nicer path through the landscape on the *right of the tree*. It is marked in blue and leads, sometimes climbing slightly, into a broad high valley with individual pines, then on through a wide field encircled by stones to a **saddle** (950 m, AWT 2.00) with bizarrely torn pines. From here you can pick out the island's steep north coast. This path would run on to Spóa, but you turn back here.

1.30 Enthusiastic climbers bear left at the **solitary tree**, following the red dots steeply uphill. Many a bead of sweat will dampen their brow before they reach a flatter area with pockets of thornbush and spurge and then a gully where a

2.10 few small, scared **kermes oaks** offer some shade. This is after all more than 1000 m above sea level. From here the rather gritty-slippery track continues uphill as far as the

2.25 rocky formations providing a windbreak on **Kalí Límni summit.** From an altitude of 1215 m asl it is possible to see as far as Rhodes and Crete on clear days (or at least, so it is said).

Return downhill by the same route and take a look into

3.00 the pots and pans in the **taverna** before resting beneath the shady leaves. Then amaze the others with the swimming things you have brought along. The inn has four rooms, in case you had to try too much of the homemade ráki.

After the well-earned rest, return along the way you came

	for 300 m, turning left towards Arh. Michaílis at the fork.

3.05 At the next fork, follow the sign indicating the **church of the Archangel Michael** to the right. From the forecourt of the new monastery you drop down into the depression. In front of the wall on the opposite slope, continue to the left along a lane through a gate to a small oasis embedded into the stone desert ④. Walk above it to the right, always following the red dots. They lead you safely between the boulders to a fenced **garden** (**P3**: N35°34.767′/ E27°08.903′). (Hidden in the oleander to the left of it is a small, refreshing waterfall!)

★

3.20

Above the garden a path takes you right, slightly uphill. Behind the garden, follow the footmarks leading into an overgrown country lane. It runs up into a little pine forest; *disregard* the markings of a narrow path going left! Spread out below in the mild afternoon light is the gently undulating landscape of the lower Lástos plain.

!!

At the top, in the pines, you come to a wide forest track (**P4**: N35°34.783′/ E27°09.240′, 710 m), where you turn down left. 50 m beyond a gate you take the path running *higher up to the right* as far as the **wide roadway** above the coastline (**P5**: N35°34.885′/ E27°09.458′). (The footpath to the St. Nicholas chapel which begins on the far side is not worthwhile.) Following the roadway up left, you are rewarded with magnificent views of the sea which you will still be dreaming of at night. In front of a farmhouse clinging to the mountain is a well. Later, below the path, the **little church** of St. Nicholas awaits you.

!!
3.35

4.00

Wandering on through the sparse pine forest, you soon see Pigádia and Apéri. At the fork next to a **water tank** (**P6**: N35°33.530/ 27°10.020′), the way home first goes down left and, after 250 m, down right. After striding through a **gravel pit**, you reach the **main road.** From here it is only 100 m to the left to get to the steps leading down through the many gardens in **Apéri** to the **Bishop's church.** Since it is almost always closed, head directly for the taverna in front of the bridge for refreshments (280 m).

4.30

4.45
4.50
5.05

⑯ A fistful of dollars

*This two to three-hour hike takes you to Óthos and
Voláda, two medieval village retreats.*
*The tour does not have any great differences in alti-
tude, mostly following tracks and one minor road.
A spectacular path leads along the steep mountain
to the church of the cross, the highlight of the hike.*
■ *5 or 6 km, difference in altitude 80 or 320 m,
easy or moderate*

AWT   In **Óthos** you should first take a look at the precious peb-
blestone floor in the Kímissis Church.

0.00   At the northern edge of the village, near the **Christós
Church**, you then take the steps leading uphill. Proceed
as far as the small street which skirts the top of the village.
Walk on up it to the right into a wide valley with sparse

0.10   pine stands. Soon the KA6 **hiking trail** turns off left. (It is
steep, gravelly and later peters out. Can only be recommended for those allergic to asphalt.)

You have just as fine a view of the coastal plain on the

0.20   small asphalt road and reach the **road** to Lástos without
effort. Go left along it and, shortly afterwards, right onto
a grey track which runs down to the cruciform-domed
church on the hill.

Leaving this track at a distance of 50m to the right, however, you soon come past a house standing directly on the
right of the track. Immediately behind it you discover a
monopáti on the right which leads down to a steep street

0.30   in the village. Drop down right to the main street in **Voláda** and then
down left, past
the car park
(left), as far as
the beautiful tav-
erna *Klimataria*
① on the right-
hand side of the
street. Before
reaching it, de-
scend the steps
on the right and
then go straight

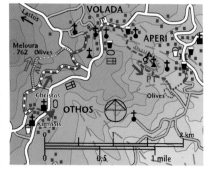

down the street, following the sign "Kastro". In the garden on the left stands a chapel.

Soon you reach the footpath, which affords a magnificent view of Apéri ②. Boldly stride along the mountain, until the path becomes a little steeper for a few meters just before the Stávros Chapel on the left. But nobody is forcing you to look down.

An acropolis stood here in ancient times, in the Middle
0.45 *Ages the now dilapidated* **castle** *of the Venetian noble family Cornaro, who ruled over Kárpathos from 1315 until 1537.*

In 1970 Greek-Americans from New Jersey had a church built here. The names of the donors are written on a marble plaque. The last one to have been immortalized donated 5 dollars.

Most visitors stroll back to Voláda from here.

Continuation to Apéri - for experienced hikers: This path into the valley is overgrown in parts, but possible to find with a keen eye. It begins, after you have walked back three minutes, in front of the soaring rock. On the left starts a stone path, which runs down into the valley in
1.10 long bends. The visible part of the path ends in the **valley floor** (**P1**: N35°32.890/ E27°09.904′).

From here you go 200 metres without a path, initially through knee-high undergrowth in the garden on the left beside the valley floor, then in the dry streambed. Where the next valley joins this one, you walk out of the valley
1.20 on a **roadway**, turn off left without a path at two sharp
1.30 bends and arrive at **Apéri.**

⑰ Another Profítis Elías

This tour takes four and a half hours and leads from Apéri to a point with a view across the Egyptian Sea before descending 500 height metres to a lovely beach. For half an hour it follows a road, otherwise tracks and paths and sometimes even without paths (long trousers are absolutely essential). Wells can be found in Apéri and on the beach as well as a cistern at the church on the peak. From May to October a taverna is open on the beach. Recommendation: It is possible to chug back comfortably by boat from the beach at Acháta, but only by informing the excursion boat "Sofia" in Pigádia before 9.30 am.

■ *12 km, difference in alt. 210 or 490 m, moderate to difficult*

AWT 0.00   Below the **road bridge in Apéri** (280 m) is a fountain. After a few metres on the ascending street you turn off right and come down to the Bishop's church with a beautiful iconostasis. If you continue downhill along the small street, you walk round the island's secondary schools, which were built from contributions by emigrants to New Jersey, the "Americánis".

The small street leads over the hill and then to the right, where there is the cemetery and, opposite it on the left –
0.10   slightly raised –, a **chapel** ①, before which you should leave the street and bear left. The narrow path leads you uphill through terraces of olive trees. In the saddle at the top you can see today's destination, the apparently invin-

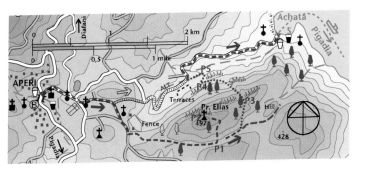

0.15 cible mountain of the prophet Elijah. From the **fork** a path runs left downhill which would also lead to the sea. (Alternative route below.)

But first you continue straight on, then slightly downhill next to a low-rise chapel (left) and left along a lane until

0.20 you reach a rather new **house** with a detached chimney standing in a fenced-off area.

!! *Immediately after the fence* you slowly ascend left between boulders, sage, juniper bushes and partly burnt pines to the flat rear side of the mountain 1. Before a green

0.50 plateau a path branches left at the **cairn** (P1: N35° 32.662'/ E27°11.730', 375 m) and leads you up a steeper,

1.05 yet wonderful stretch through junipers to the **summit of**
★ **Profítis Elías** (P2: N35°32.909'/ E27°11.728'; 490 m).

> *The prophet Elijah, the Christian successor to the Greek sun god Helios, is the standard saint on the high island mountains closest to the sun. A small chapel can almost always be found on the peaks.*

The rest of the way can be seen clearly from here: almost due east, and a bit lower down, is a wide gap and behind it a plateau with trees. That is where the descent down the steeper side of the mountain begins.

From the peak, first return the way you came to get to the

1.20 **high valley** (AWT 0.50 on the ascent).

> *Alternative:* The way down to the valley described below is mainly without paths and moderately steep, but considerably shorter. The final 50 metres are very thorny and cannot be negotiated in shorts!

The easier but longer way to the bay is to walk back along the same path for 45 minutes to the fork (AWT 0.15) and from there down to the right for a further

      45 minutes, at the end along the road to the beach.

1.20 At the **cairn** you go left onto a trekking path which traverses the high valley ③. 300 m before the round cone-shaped hill you go left without a path and then right along the hillside on the left. Where the plain falls away, you should follow the red dots leading gently uphill to

1.35 the **wide gap**. (P3: N35°32.977'/ E27°11.988', 385 m) ④. Here the trees which one could already see from above provide a perfect spot to have a picnic.

From the gap you descend right, keeping to the fall line, and pass a wide ridge of rock on your right. Continue descending in the same direction, 50 m away from a row of rocks (right), behind which follows an abrupt drop. The lower row of large pines (225 m) stays on your left. Further down you turn left above a rocky slope and come in-

2.15 to another **wide gap** between two rock faces (**P4:** N35° 33.058'/ E27°11.543', 160 m). One face is above you on the left, the other down to your right. Here a belt of prickly bushes blocks the way down, so you must press yourself right up against the bare rock in order to reach the streambed (**P5:** N35°33.096'/ E27°11.520). Because it is

2.25 *impassable downstream,* go left to the **road**. Phew! What a relief!

While you are walking down, look up at the cliff you have conquered, and you will feel like Edmund Hillary. The

2.55 other bathers at the **beach in Acháta** ④ had an easier
OW time getting here.

Even when Captain Vassilis zooms round the corner with his "Sofia", you needn't hurry. His other guests also dive into the clear blue water before he steers his boat back to Pigádia.

⑱ A Day for Swimming

This will be a relaxing day. Just three hours along the gently curving stretch of beautiful coastline south of Diafáni – or a little longer when allowance is made for extended stops for a swim and picnic.
■ *8 km, difference in altitude 60 m, easy*

AWT 0.00	From the figure of the **Diafáni fisherman's wife** sadly gazing out to sea we saunter south along the harbour as far as a slipway (left), where we go right along a path leading through all manner of nautical bits and pieces and
0.05	then up left to a **chapel** (right).
	We take the roadway going left. Having passed Cape Thalasopoúnda, it runs downhill. Shortly before reaching the bottom of the valley (**P1**: N35°45.026′/E27°12.798′), we leave the roadway at the cairn, entering a path on the left
0.10	and traversing a **gully**.
0.20	For ten minutes the path leads us through olive gardens as far as a tiny **bathing place** in a hollow (**P2**: N35°44.765′/ E27°12.871′). From there we ascend a trekking
0.30	path to the **roadway** (50 m), which we take for nine minutes to the left.
!!	We pass three gullies which descend into the sea; to the left of the fourth one are *three small olive terraces. 60 metres beyond them* (**P3**: N35°44.384′/ E27°12.795′) we turn
0.40	**left** off the roadway into a *narrow path* which again leads through a gully ①. 100 m after a house (right, with concrete table) we traverse another valley. Back up on the
0.50	**roadway** we go left, right at the fork and already after 30 m onto a path going left! It leads through a small olive

grove to a hill above the sea. It becomes narrower here and winds its way down steeply into a wide valley. The **beach of Papas Mínas** ☑ (P4: N35°44.180'/E27°13.061') is on the left. If the dark grey slate slabs are too hot to lie on, they can be cooled with plastic bags full of sea water. We return the same way we came, only this time with a view of Mount Orkili (710 m). Naturally we remember the two branch-offs from the roadway. Prior to entering Diafáni, we turn off to the right into the valley before the first chapel and stride into the **harbour** full of vim and vigour.

0.55

1.50

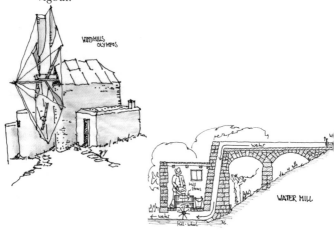

WINDMILLS OLYMPOS

WATER MILL

⑲ A solitary chapel

This three to four-hour ascent from Diafáni to Ólympos leads through deserted hilly country with distant views of the sea. Beside the well marked path is not only an ancient chapel, but also a spring. Apart from the last 30 minutes on a road the hike takes you along solitary paths.

■ *12 km, difference in alt. 325 m, moderate to difficult*

▷ *Map see previous page*

AWT 0.00	From the **well** in **Diafáni** harbour you walk up past the taverna Coralis, where the landlord Michalis is known to reach for his lyra in the evenings. Immediately behind it you ascend a long stairway leading left up to the St. Nicolas Church. From there you go on up left and, on the roadway, first right, then left. Having passed between windmill and cemetery, you hug the top of Diafáni.
!! 0.10	Later, already in the woods, the roadway makes a left turn ①. *Just before that* you leave the roadway at the hand-painted sign "Melena", **climbing right** into a narrow slate path which ascends through sparse pine woods ②.
0.20	From a **hilltop** (150 m) you look across a superbly solitary, green hilly landscape and far over the blue sea.
0.25	Having reached the **crest** (**P1**: N35°44.800'/ E27°12.324'), you see a roadway on the right in a valley ③ and drop down to it. Making your way carefully down the slippery slate and through an **olive grove**, you reach the roadway.
0.30	It is the local hiking trail "7b", which you follow to the left.

In the valley floor you will find plenty of water, collected in a small reservoir. Further up reeds and oleander line the path winding its way uphill. Later a solitary grey chapel comes into view in the hills .

0.55   When you are below this chapel, a path branches right off the roadway. Via an olive grove it first leads you on level ground, then rises up to the ancient **Áyios Konstantínos chapel**, now only in a makeshift state of repair (**P2:** N35° 44.414'/ E27°11.839'; 210 m).

1.10   Walk back 40 m, then left and on uphill. The path along slippery slate is quite strenuous. In the **saddle** (**P3:** N35° 44.257'/ E27°11.697'; 325 m) you are relieved to be able to go downhill again. Later, to the left of the path, is a dry

1.20   streambed, which you traverse in order to reach a **roadway** (**P4:** N35°44.220'/ E27°11.361'; 290 m).

After two minutes you are on the main road, which leads left to Pigádia. Proceed right down it and later, at the

1.35   **fork**, left. Ólympos has long since come into view.

You could descend into the valley across terraces and take the wide stone path up the other side. But that was surely enough up and down for one day. While the road may not be quite in keeping with a hike, it does bring you

1.50   faster to **Ólympos.** The day trippers are gradually having to drift back to the bus, so you are soon alone in the steep alleys of the wonderful old mountain village. To spend the evening here is a really special experience – assuming one has organized the return journey.

⑳ A Day Excursion

This walk is a chance for those who come from Pigádia by ship for a day, in particular, to "stretch their legs". After visiting Ólympos, it is possible to stroll through a green valley back down to the ship in Diafáni in two hours.
This lovely route is easy to find and even has a well along the way.

■ *6 km, difference in alt. 245 m, easy to moderate*

AWT
0.00   Picturesque windmills are lined up along the edge of the slope in **Ólympos** (245 m), but the **taverna "Milos"** or "Windmill", at the bottom of the slope is the only one to have covered blades. From here, you go down several steps on the side facing away from the sea in an arc to the right and come to a roadway below the houses. Further

0.05   down it, turn off sharply **to the left.** 50 m further on, a trekking path to the right leads below a barrel-vaulted church ☐ to the confluence of two streams and, there, across the roadway. Next to the smaller stream on the left you go uphill and then downhill again, where you see a

0.15   walled **well** (**P1:** N35°44.766'/ E27°10.614') and, above it on the right, a hill chapel. Wander left up the steambed

0.20   until **markings** guide you up to the right. Despite all this path-finding, do not forget to look back!

Later you cross the dry-bed again and come to a fork, where you head up to the right and immediately come to a pump building on the left beside the dry-bed. It is only a

0.25   few steps from there up to the **road.**

0.35   Go left up the road and, at the **saddle** (240 m), 20 m up-

hill at the left turn-off You quickly discover the trekking path leading steeply downwards to the right. At the bottom, you cross the road and walk further downhill in the dry-bed until you come to a **culvert** beneath the road.

0.45

After crossing over or under the road, you see pines lining the continuation along the slaty riverbed ②. It is a wonderful path, even offering a **well** (right). At the confluence with a stream coming down from the left you later discover an old, water-driven **grain mill** at the foot of the slope on the left. It hasn't ground grain for a long time. Water fell from the upright pipe into the building attached below, which housed the water wheel and above it the two horizontal millstones. (Sketch on page 74)

0.55

1.05

1.10

Further down the riverbed you come to a **track** leading to the village of Diafáni. The new cement walls here were built to prevent another flood catastrophe like the one in October 1994. You reach the village along the wide cement canal, which you leave to the left in the old part and continue straight on to the **jetty in Diafáni.** However, the inn-keepers know how to prevent you from boarding the ship right away.

1.25

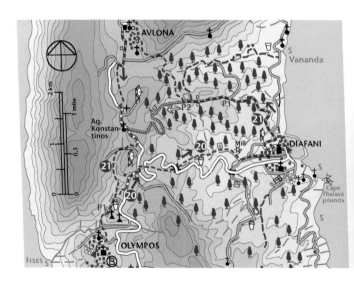

㉑ The Ascent to Ólympos

This four-hour hike shows the picturesque village Ólympos against the backdrop of the majestic mountains. The first sight of Ólympos will remain unforgettable. From Diafáni, the route follows a forest track and an old kalderími to the village of Avlóna, which seems lost in time. Following refreshments there, the tour continues up along one of the loveliest paths on the islands to Ólympos.
At AWT 0.45 it is possible to branch off on an alternative circuit with a swim.
■ *11 km, difference in alt. 260 m, moderate to difficult*

▷ *See map on previous page.*

AWT	
0.00	From the **jetty in Diafáni**, walk north for 50 metres, turn off inland (to the left) at the baking oven and immediately afterwards continue uphill to the right. At the next fork, bear uphill to the left along a wide concrete road leading out of the village. Where it forks, go straight
0.08	ahead, past **antennas** (left), until you come to the next
0.12	**fork** in front of a circular water tank.

You naturally take the narrower path leading left up through a sparse pine forest. Up at the top the air blows like in a wind tunnel. Bending to the left, you struggle against the wind – something the trees have long since given up doing.

0.35 At a **right turn-off** (**P1**: N35°45.878'/ E27°11.782') you go to the left and then stroll along above a valley on almost level ground ☐. A little later you change to the other

side of the hill and look down into a valley on the right. After walking between the ruins of two houses, you come
0.45 to a **walled olive grove** on the right (**P2**: N35°45.892'/ E27°11.317', 235 m).

> *Short cut:* By staying on the roadway, you avoid Avlónas and arrive directly at the church Ayios Konstantinos.

> *Alternative:* Just below the grove a very lovely, well-marked path leads through pine forests and streambeds to the **beach at Vanánda** in 35 minutes. For a description, see ㉒ after AWT 3.35.

0.45 *Above* the walled grove, your route branches off to the right. At first walking beneath pines, you later use a flagstone path from times long past. It meanders harmoniously across the plateau ②, traverses a hollow, passes
1.00 through a **gate** and is interrupted shortly after that by a new roadway. Walk along it to the left for 200 m and then up to the right. On the left, fields nestle in the high valley.

1.10 The village of **Avlóna** (290 m) is located behind the hill.

> *The name means "small valley". Time seems to have stood still here. Narrow lanes curve round the houses; every now and again you discover an old draw well and an alóni, or threshing area. Everything is still in working order. This "outer village" is only inhabited at harvest time. A taverna is sometimes open and it is a relief to find that the drinks come out of a modern refrigerator.*

1.10 From the taverna, continue to the south, towards the antennas, along the roadway. Friendly countrywomen in old traditional costumes will wave to you from the fields. The roadway ascends slowly and, after eight minutes, in the first hair-pin bend to the right, you will find the familiar red signs indicating the old paths. Continue straight on across the bottom of the valley along the beautiful flagstone path, later through a gate and up to the ridge. You meet up with the **road** again there and quickly reach the **Chapel of Constantine** (260 m) ③ by walking along it to the left. The church is situated in majestic mountain scenery and affords a fantastic view of Ólympos.

1.30
1.35

Walk down the road and, after three minutes, 40 m beyond a culvert, you see the beginning of the old footpath which zigzags steeply downhill. The views you get here are among the most spectacular in the Aegean ④. Behind Ólympos steep cliffs rise up as in a dream landscape. It is the kind of sight you can also sometimes find in the Andes.

★

Further down you go 50 m to the right along the transversal **roadway** and, initially in the **streambed**, later to the right above it, proceed straight on. Having crossed the streambed, you continue on its left side. Again walking in the streambed, you see, beneath a hill chapel, a walled spring on the left – that is where you leave the streambed to the right. Beneath Ólympos **steps** lead up to a roadway. Walk along it to the left for 50 m and then to the right up to the magnificent village of **Ólympos**, which is no longer so crowded as evening approaches. Down below the sea glitters.

1.45
2.00

2.15

2.25

▷ The taverna in **Avlóna** has new **rooms for guests** with traditional furnishings and soufás, Kárpathos-style platform beds. Waking up in this secluded village is a very special experience (tel. 22450-51046).

▷ The balconies of the fancifully constructed **boarding house** "Glaros" at Diafáni are especially suitable for a lazy day (tel. 22450-51501).

㉒ The Vanished City

This seven-hour hike, probably the most impressive on Kárpathos, is especially memorable in spring – but does require a certain degree of stamina! It mostly follows paths without steep ascents. Avlóna offers places to stop and even to stay overnight (see p. 81). Among the many items of equipment to take along is a torch.
An elegant short-cut would be to arrange to be picked up by a boat in Vroukoúnda! (see p.92) Or to take a taxi to the Konstantínos chapel or to Avlóna.
■ *20 km, difference in altitude 300 m, difficult*

AWT 0.00 Nimbly jumping off the bus at the **turn-off to Avlóna**, you walk up to the right along the asphalt road and leave the beautiful mountain village of Ólympos behind you. Where the power lines approach the road on the left, you can select a footpath running down below as a short-cut.

0.15 Soon you reach the **Áyios Konstantínos chapel**, which offers the loveliest view of Ólympos, and then continue along the road, which later leads downhill. Opposite the gravel pit (left), you pass through a gate to reach the old mule track leading down to Avlóna, which soon comes into view. It is a wonderful stroll, and later you turn right

0.35 on the concrete road to arrive at **Avlóna** ① (280 m, p. 80). You pass a village taverna (right) on "main street". Walking along the wide lane for another five minutes, in several bends through fertile land, always following the signs

0.45 for "Vroukounda", you enter a portal made of gigantic **fig trees** on the left ② (**P1:** N35°46.636'/ E27°10.707').

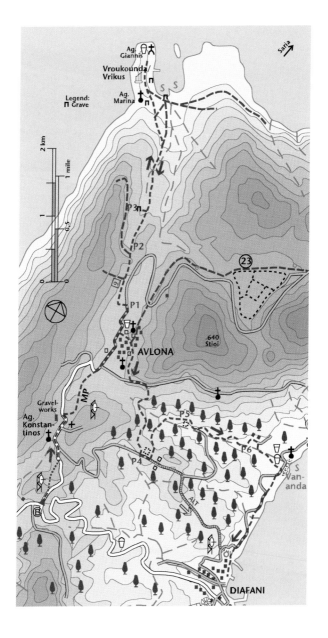

The stone barriers along a monopáti lead you towards the sea, at first slightly uphill. At an indistinct fork you go right and, after 200 m, through another **gate** in the saddle (**P2:** N35°46.937'/ E27°10.539'). The fields are no longer cultivated; the area becomes more and more isolated. But the blue sea entices you downwards – partly on artistically constructed kalderímis, partly on gravel paths. A sign points to an ancient **tomb** with shield reliefs 100 m to the left of the path (**P3:** N35°47.375'/ E27°10.421'). The panorama extends from the sister island Saría on the right to the Vroukoúnda peninsula, resembling a table mountain, in front on the left ③. Proceed laboriously down the steep gravel path to the coastal plain.

In front of the peninsula on the left between the cliffs is the Ayía Marína chapel, into which ancient building components have been incorporated.

On the main path you notice a massive boulder on the left, full of holes like a tooth with cavities and sheltering recesses for graves. Climb up the steps to the table mountain. Towering up on the left are the enormous square stone walls of the ancient city.

*In Antiquity **the city of Vríkous** stood on the plateau. It was one of four Dorian cities on Kárpathos and Saría and was founded 3000 years ago. It seems probable that a Mycenaean settlement was located at this easily defensible place even earlier. The city was still inhabited in Byzantine and Venetian times, but was then probably abandoned due to frequent attacks by pirates.*

Everything has vanished. The city ground plan with alleys and houses can no longer be discerned, as many of the medium-high walls have been used to build goat pens.

0.55

1.10

1.40

1.50 Another unusual sight awaits you at the end of the peninsula: the underground **chapel of Áyios Giánnis**. The chancel is divided by two ancient columns; water drips into the cross-shaped marble baptismal font from the ceiling. The church anniversary festival is on August 28 and 29. The atmosphere is indescribable when hundreds of candles are burning down here.

It is a long trek back, so be sure to fill up with fresh water beside the chapel. Behind the sandy-pebbly beach are more grave chambers in the cliffs, all facing towards the sunrise; they used to be closed by stone slabs. From the beach, take the same way back. First climb 300 metres to
2.50 the **saddle** and then on to **Avlóna**.

3.05 *Alternative:* If you want to go to Ólympos from here, use ㉑.

200 m beyond the taverna, after a well, turn left into a lane, zigzag up the hill and then turn to the right. At the southern end of the village you see the barrel-vaulted chapel of Áyios Nikoláos ④, which you pass before meet-
3.15 ing a **kalderími**. Walk left along the country lane which
3.20 soon follows for 150 m, where you will find **signs** on the right leading down to the continuation of the kalderími. It first leads through the hollow, then over a hilltop and down to the shady pine forest with a fragrant aroma.

3.35 Walk round a **walled olive grove** (left) (**P4:** N35°45.892'/ E27°11.317', 245 m) and then 50 m left down the wide forest track.

Short Cut: If you stay on the wide forest track and later disregard a *turn-off to the left,* not walking downhill to the left until after the antennas of **Diafáni**, you can order something to drink at the harbour 40 minutes later. Although the two short cuts for hikers are signposted, they are quite steep.

3.35 The more romantic way, though, turns off to the left be-
3.45 low the walled olive grove. You walk downhill over slaty
!! ground beneath pines. Traverse the **bottom of the valley** and pay careful attention to the *directional arrows* which have been carefully set up there. Head towards the sea on the left above the streambed. Passing another walled
3.50 **olive grove** (**P5:** N35°46.160'/ E27°11.658'), you later
3.55 come to the **streambed** again. Ignore the roadway there. Walk on the left above the streambed for a while, then to the right of it for five minutes. When you see a shed on

4.10 the left of the slope, leave the streambed to the left (**P6:** N35°46.257'/ E27°12.268') and after ten metres turn up-hill to the left again into **olive terraces** shortly after-wards. After the **house** (left) at the "Odos Kanari", turn to the right into the streambed again and leave it after 50 m,
4.15 going up to the right to reach the **beach at Vanánda**, which has a well and a kind of garden restaurant.

4.40 To return, use the roadway briefly and take four short-cut footpaths along the rocky cliff to reach **Diafáni.**

Translation of special words for hikers

English	Français	Italiano	Nederlands	Svenska
boulder	bloc de rocher	masso	Rotsblok	klippblock
cairn	marquage	segnalato di pietre	Markeringssteen	vägmärke
cleft, ditch, dip	fossé	fosso	Sloot	sänka
crest, ridge	crête	cresta	Bergkam	bergskam
culvert	passage d'eau	passagio	Water buis	vattenledning
defile	chemin creux	strada incassata	Holleweg	hålväg
ford	gué	guado	Wad	vadställe
fork, turn off	bifurcation	bifurcazione	Wegsplitsing	vägskäl
gap	brèche	breccia	Bres	inskärning
glade, clearing	clairière	radura	Open plek in bos	glänta
gorge, ravine	gorge, ravine	abisso	Kloof, Ravijn	ravin
gravel	pierraille	ghiaia	Steengruis	stenskärvor
grove	bosquet	bosco	Bosschage	lund
gully, incision	cours d'eau	letto di fiume	Waterloop	vattendrag
heath	bruyère	brughiera	Heide	hed
hollow	dépression	depressione	Glooiing	sänka
incline	pente	pendio	Helling	sluttning
past	près de	accanto a	naast	jämte
pebble	caillou	ciottolo	Kiezel	grus
pen	bergerie	stalla ovile	Stal	stall
rift	fossée	fosso	Sloot	sänka
rim	bords	orlo	Rand	kant
rubble, scree	éboulis	ditriti	Steengruis	stenar
saddle	crête	sella	Bergrug	bergsrygg
schist	schiste	scisto	Leisteen	skiffer
scrub	fourré	sterpaglia	Doornbos	snår
slope	pente	pendio	Helling	sluttning
stream bed	lit	letto di fiume	Waterloop	vattendrag
strenuous	fatigant	faticoso	inspannend	ansträngande
well	puits	pozzo	Bron	brunn

German version ISBN 978-3-9814047-0-8

㉓ Pretty Well Alone

Those who wish to go it alone on this hike, which takes four hours in one direction, should take along a mobile phone and whatever else is necessary, for they will not meet a soul for hours. While water can be found at the start and end of the tour, the route only has markings (OL8) at the beginning.
The tour is commendable not only on account of the landscape, but also the beautiful old paths. It is advisable to do one leg by boat (see p. 92).

■ *11 km, difference in altitude 430 m, difficult*

Avlóna – Trístomo

AWT

0.00 The most convenient place to start the tour is in **Avlóna**. In front of the **taverna**, take the lane on the right, go left after 80 m and follow the red dots which lead out of the village to a monopáti, where you see a large sign to Trístomo. After a gate the lane becomes a trekking path which

0.08 **crosses a roadway** shortly afterwards. The following path, subsequently with flagstones, runs up the slope to the right. The walled fields in the valley are the island's granary. Many of the inhabitants of Olympos and Diafáni have fields here.

Then, turning your back to the valley, you pass a concrete

0.20 trough on the right and **walk down** to the fertile valley of Achórdea ①. In front of the walls round the fields a

0.25 weathered **sign** (**P1:** N35°47.120'/ E27°11.308') directs you to the left, always staying next to the wall. A water hose accompanies you.

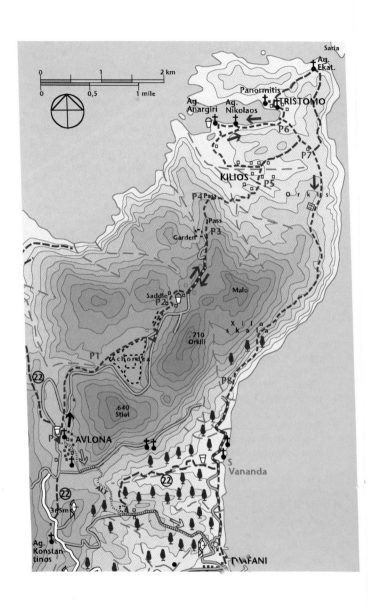

0.40   At the end of the walls is another concrete **trough.** From there, proceed up the country lane for four to five min-

0.45   utes, but then turn left at a large **boulder** (30 m left) marked in blue and follow the trekking path which runs parallel to the lane. Between the field walls and the remains of some buildings, you reach the saddle (420 m)

1.00   and a **cistern** (**P2:** N35°47.847'/ E27°12.184'). Shortly afterwards, between two troughs, you come to a roadway,

1.05   which you follow as far as a **sharp left-hand bend.**

      A marked trekking path leads straight ahead downhill and, after a further 30 m of lane, runs to the right above a

1.10   **garden** (**P3:** N35°48.156'/ E27°12.431'). Walking down a

★   wonderful, partly flagstone path ②, with spectacular views, you see the plains of Kilíos and the island of Saría

1.25   from the last **hilltop** ③ (**P4:** N35°48.567'/ E27°12.453', 270 m).

      The carefully laid flagstone path zigzags down to the fertile plains. They were cultivated up until 40 years ago.

1.45   At the bottom, cross the first dry-bed with a **short turn** to the left (**P5:** N35°48.455'/ E27°12.784, 70 m) and, after two minutes, turn downhill to the left in the second. On the right side of the path are the ruins of the houses of the village of Kilíos, which was not visible from the sea. Near the sea, leave the field walls and the pond on the left and walk over a small hill, where you see Ayíi Anargíri chapel up on the left. Above the bay with the St. Nicholas chapel ④ you

2.20   proceed to **Trístomo** (**P4:** N35°49.253'/ E27°13.325').

OW   The inhabitants have moved away and left behind empty buildings. A lonely place.

      Now you have the choice of **two different ways** of walking back.

Return route to Díafani along the coast

This route (OL 11) along the cliffs above the shore partly follows a narrow path which was restored in 2005. The ground underneath is slaty and partly slippery. Whoever chooses this way must be absolutely sure-footed and have a head for heights. Moreover the weather should not be too windy.
On the plus side this route affords spectacular views and a refreshing swim in Vanánda.
■ *10 km, difference in altitude 170 m, difficult*

AWT
2.20

In **Trístomo** you set off uphill at the metal board showing the way to Diafáni, to the right of the animal enclosure. Climb up steeply to the right between two walls, then left through a gap in the wall and immediately right again. A path leads diagonally up the slope between the boulders, bringing you to the ruins of a house (right) at the top. Looking into the next valley, you go to the left and, after

2.45

80 m, come to a **fork** (**P7:** N 35°48.976′/ E 27°13.689′; 170 m). The way to the left leads to St. Catherine's chapel and the northernmost point on Kárpathos, Cape Stenó.
You walk to the right here and then on the same level along the hillside, picking out Kilíos valley and your out-

2.55

ward route on the right. Soon you reach a **saddle.** The sea below you, the descent begins.
For 20 minutes you cross the no longer cultivated fields of Orkis. On clear days it is possible to look across to Rhodes

✓

and Chálki. Then you descend more steeply and all eyes are on the path.

4.00

The **stone steps** are a landmark. They were originally

made of wood and gave the region its name, Xilóskala, wooden stairs. After that you traverse an area with size-able boulders (**P8:** N 35°47.284'/ E 27°12.973'). Pines give some shade until you reach a wide path again ⑤. The path

✓
✓

4.30
4.50   ends at a shed (right) and becomes a **roadway**, which runs down to **Vanánda**. There you can have a swim and, if you must, take a drink in the bizarre bar beneath trees.

5.10   Continue along the shore to **Diafáni** (see p.86)

Return route to Avlóna keeping inland

This is the already described outward route. For those who came by boat, the first time indication applies.

0.00/
2.20   From abandoned **Trístomo**, keep to the shore, turn right to the St. Nicholas chapel and continue to the chapel of

0.15/
2.35   **Ayíi Anargíri** with cistern and a chance to have a swim From there, walk over the small hill, then on the left of the pond and, after a ruin, continue round the field walls

0.20/
2.40   in a curve to the right until you come to the **ruins of a house** (left), where you go slightly uphill.

The blue markings found here later lead you downhill to a place where two valleys meet. Follow the left valley up-hill, with the ruins of the houses in the abandoned village

0.40/
3.00   Kilíos on the left, then later two big **fig trees** on the right, where you directly continue up to the right. Two minutes later, cross a dry-bed diagonally off towards the left (**P5:** N35°48.455'/ E27°12.784') and cheerfully begin the steep ascent.

Soon you come to a large boulder next to a house. The zigzag path with steps is still the only connection to

1.05/
3.25   Ólympos by land. The ascent to the **first hilltop** (**P4:** N35°48.567'/ E27°12.453', 270 m) requires the most en-

1.20/
3.40   durance. A less steep stretch follows to the next **pass** (380 m). From here you see a deserted, walled garden (right)

1.25/
3.45   and, behind it, the beginning of a **roadway**, which you then take, cutting off a bend after 20 m. Walk uphill along the roadway and across the hilltop until it forks at two

1.35/
3.55   **concrete troughs** near some walls.
Go to the right here, then immediately to the left, past a cistern (**P2:** N35°47.847'/ E27°12.184'), and on to the right near the walls. At 420 m above sea-level, this is high-

est point on the tour. Now descend between field walls to- wards the Achórdea plain.

1.50/ At a **boulder** with blue markings, change to the left onto
4.10 the roadway running downhill. It forks at a trough (right) – go on the right of the walls alongside the water hose. At the end of the walls, turn right at the **signpost** (left) (**P1**: N35°47.120'/ E27°11.308') and walk straight uphill along a wide flagstone path. Down on the right is a gorge; later,

2.10/ on the left, is another **trough.**
4.30 Fields appear in front of you. After a gate, walk to the left, and soon you see Avlóna ⑥ with its antennas. Cross over the roadway which has for so long accompanied you in- visibly higher up, in order to reach the "outside village" of

2.15/ **Avlóna** (**P**: N35°46.469'/ E27°10.832', 285 m), which is
4.35 only inhabited at harvest time. Sometimes you can get something to eat and drink here; you could have a taxi
OW pick you up here.

2.35/ If you want to wander on to **Diafáni**, follow ㉒, but
4.55 preferably taking the alternative as a short-cut (AWT
RT 3.35). This takes an hour.

㉑ leads to **Ólympos** beginning at AWT 1.10.

▶ Captain Nikos Orphános can take hikers **to Trístomo or Saría by boat** or fetch them there. His office is at the harbour, tel. 22450-51410.
Vasílis Baláskas also plies this route.

▶ **Individual hikers** sometimes have a cheaper option: if you contact the captain of the **excursion boat**, "Karpathos II", to Saría a day in advance, you can arrange to be let off in Trístomo. The disadvantage is that you won't arrive there until 11.15 am in the midday heat.

㉔ On Saría

As Saría has not been permanently inhabited for 30 years, it only has footpaths. One of them runs from the south to the north of the varied island in four to five hours. The journey there and back is by private boat (see p. 92). Cisterns are to be found at the start and end of the almost shadeless route.

■ **11 km, difference in alt. 275 m, moderate to difficult**

AWT
0.00

The strait between Kárpathos and Saría is just 150 m wide. After the crossing the boat lets walkers off at **Iaplós Beach.**
Walking to the right along the beach, you head towards the Áyios Spirídon chapel and, before reaching it, up through the gaps in the field walls on the left. A rather indistinct path ascends the right side of the hill.

0.20

After passing through a gate beyond the **hilltop** (150 m), you reach a cistern (**P1**: N35°50.783'/ E27°14.023'). Shortly after that you disregard a shed on the right and cross an olive grove ① on the Pila plain. Before the path climbs, it runs past another **shed** and, halfway up, joins a path which comes from the left (**P2**: N35°51.209'/ E27°14.017').

0.30

0.40
0.45

On the hilltop you pass a **walled olive grove** (right) and then arrive at the **Andreas Chapel** ② (**P3**: N35°51.400'/ E27°14.055', 210 m).
Past a shed (right) you drop into the hollow, go right along the walled olive grove and up an indistinct path again. At the top is a further olive grove on the right. In the next hollow the same procedure: past the right-hand

1.00

side of the walled olive grove, but then up wide **stone**

steps followed by a fairly long flat stretch ③. A house with a wall frieze gives an idea of how life used to be here: Spartan – but with a regal panorama (**P4**: N35°51.851'/ E27°13.936').

Thereafter the terrain falls away slightly into a hollow with a walled field, but we stay halfway up the slope and find a few shade providers at last. The path ascends again slightly and passes an enormous cave. At the top it zigzags through the rocks; those with a fear of heights had better not look down at the sea. Immediately after

1.40 that you reach the **Alonás plateau** (**P5**: N35°52.597'/ E27°13.740', 275 m).

After 100 m the path forks – we go left. Having strolled along on the same level for a while, you turn right into a gorge and climb back up the opposite slope. At the top you see the next destinations: the abandoned village of Árgos and, over to the right in the cliffs, the white Zacharias chapel. A gravel path leads us to the village and

2.10 **forks** below it (**P6**: N 35°53.295'/ E 27°13.396').

> ***Short cut:*** Go right here and reach **Palátia bay** in 15 min.

From the **fork** continue uphill to

2.10 dilapidated **Árgos**, which has been abandoned for about 30 years. The houses are partly still furnished as the owners from Diafáni keep goats here.

After walking through the village, turn right onto a path leading towards a solitary **fig tree**. Walk 30 m around and above it and then,

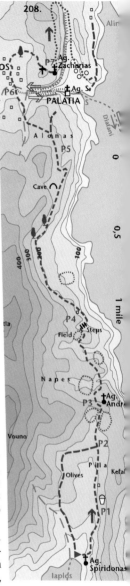

2.15   bearing right, saunter up the hill. You pass a toppled **cross**

2.25   at the summit and then see the white **church of Áyios Zacharias (P7:** N35°53.319′/ E27°13.714′) ②. On September 5 the families of the former inhabitants meet here for the church anniversary festival.

From the church you continue north without a path along the steep hillside, then over rising ground. Now it is only another 300 m until you find a suitable point to attempt

3.05   the **descent** into the high valley on the right – between cliffs and without a path and even on the seat of your

3.15   pants at times. Keep to the right to reach the **middle of the valley** and continue right (south) to reach the way out of the valley again. A long time ago this area was cultivated. Walls alongside the fields testify to this. Farming must have been terribly laborious – stones, nothing but stones.

3.30   At the end of the level area you come to **house ruins** and go left round the hill. Towering up there are large circular, beehive-like remains of houses, called "palaces" ("palátia"). They are said to have been built by Syrian pirates 600 years ago. They could also be early Christian graves. In the lower valley connecting to here, follow a path down to

3.40   **Palátia bay.** Already during Doric times, a city existed here.

Walk of three hours around Palátia: Walk through the tamarisk trees and up the streambed. After a few metres, the hidden chapel of Sophia comes into view on the left. It was originally much larger and allegedly had 101 doors. Then transverse the picturesque gorge. A plateau extends behind it, where the **path forks (P6:** N35°53.295′/ E27° 13.396′). From there you follow the description above from AWT 2.10 up to the right.

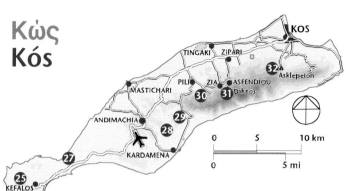

Κώς
Kós

Since ancient times the home of Hippocrates is used to hosting guests. The elegant holiday and spa guests of the olden days have now been replaced by tourists from all over Europe who are attracted by the beautiful, kilometre-long sandy beaches. In addition, though, the city of Kós, with its interesting monuments from the past 3000 years, is well worth visiting. It is a very special kind of open air museum.

Hikers can expect an extensive network of trails, which make it possible to undertake many intensive explorations of the island. Of topographical interest and most suitable for hiking are the hilly Kéfalos peninsula, which is of volcanic origin, and the wooded Dikéos mountain range, the elongated island's backbone. In the south it soars up out of the sea, in the north it peters out gently at the waterside. Especially in the mountains it is possible to find wells the whole year through. This is where the island's vegetation is at its most luscious, thanks to the abundant supply of water. The flat north coast offers long beaches and is better discovered by bicycle.

Since 2009 the Austrian Kompass publishing house has issued a map on a scale of 1:50,000, also for the other islands in the southern Dodecanese.

Thanks to the efficient public bus system it is easy to reach the starting points of the walks described here. Tours 25 and 30 can be especially recommended. Some walks on Nísyros and Psérimos are possible on day excursions.

㉕ Sound of the sea

Today we want to experience the windy northwest coast of Kós. Half the three-and-a-half hour trek runs along coastal paths or directly beside the water. The way to the sea is not difficult to find, but offers neither woods nor wells. Not until we reach the beach taverna "Áyios Theólogos" can we expect shade, food and drink.

■ *12 km, difference in altitude 100 m, moderate*

AWT	From the **bus station in Kéfalos** you walk uphill at the
0.00	left turn and enter the fourth street on the right before the childrens' playground. After 30 m you take the street going left. At the fork in front of a building yard you keep
0.05	left and pass a **marble workshop** (left). Up on the ridge the wind rotors turn, something the abandoned windmill on the left can no longer do. Having twice passed through
0.15	a dip, you turn – at the top again – left into a **street** (**P1**: N36°44.739'/ E26°56.952').
	After the asphalt has become sand, the roadway leads past the substation of the rotors (right) and over a ridge. Hav-
0.20	ing gone straight ahead at the following **crossroads** (left a cattle trough) you head in the direction of the sea. Four terraced houses stand above a fork, where you continue straight on. After a dip comes another fork, beside which
0.30	is a **fenced-in house** in an olive grove on the left (**P2**: N36°44.462'/ E26°56.053'). Here you go right and, after 100 m, proceed left on the same level at the fork. At a cattle trough you take the country lane down left.
	30 m *before a sharp right bend* you leave the lane, turning

!!	left into a path (**P3:** N36°44.443'/ E26°55.749'). This first leads through a gap before turning towards the sea. Most-
0.50	ly without a path, you finally reach a **bay** (**P4:** N36° 44.429'/ E26°55.414'), on either side of which lie further deserted beaches ①.
★	Time for a break!
	Sauntering beside the water, accompanied by the sound of the sea, we gradually set off on the rest of the way. First for twelve minutes along coastal paths traversing moorland above the pumice cliffs, then 80 m along a roadway and later back along distinct paths through bushes. After
1.15	a **deep ravine** it is also possible to walk on the strand itself ②.
1.35	At a **narrow point** you may have to take off your boots or place new stepping stones. Further on you unfortunately have to leave the strand via one of the two rifts leading up to the paths at the top, as the waves break directly against the rocks. At the top you eventually come to a roadway
1.45	and, going right, arrive at the wide **strand of Káta.** From
2.05	there it is not far to the **Áyios Theólogos taverna** (**P5:** N36°42.839'/ E 26°55.347').
	The motorists gathered there would surely have been glad to experience so many deserted beaches!

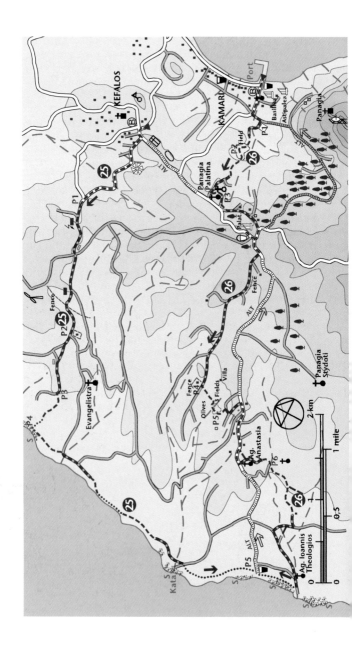

㉖ Above the Sheep's Head

Seen from the air, the western end of Kos looks like a sheep's head – which is probably the reason for the Greek name "Kéfalos" or "head". This walking tour takes over four hours one way and mainly leads along field tracks from Kamári across the high ridge to the wildly romantic westcoast – and ends at a good taverna. Orientation is rather difficult in places. Along the way you come to the idyllic ruins of a church and a dilapidated theatre. If you want to enjoy a wonderful sunset over the sea, you should get a taxi to fetch you from the taverna "Theológos" (22420-71428 or -71596, please check beforehand!). It is also possible to start in Kéfalos village, cutting 15 minutes off the tour.

■ *13 km, alt. difference 155 m, moderate to difficult*

▷ *Map see previous page.*

AWT **Short cut:** If you set out from Kéfalos, you take the street running south, past the cemetery and the sports area, to the church of Panagía Palatianí, which is situated on an elevation to the left of the street (= AWT 0.30).

0.00 From the **harbour in Kamári**, take the street running inland from the recommendable restaurant "Fáros" and
0.08 turn left at the second **turn-off**, immediately before the street goes uphill, onto a roadway on the left. Before the large raised concrete square (**P1**: N36°44.018'/ E26° 57.906') you go right ①, at once noticing a small altar on the left. In front of the white cliffs you proceed right into

the valley, along an olive grove (right), until the trail ends at a field. Walk up across the field without a track, first right, then left. After 20m, on the upper plateau, you use pumice-stone steps on the right ② and ascend four metres (**P2:** N 36°44.119′/ E26°57.645′). From there a well-beaten track leads uphill across the terraces until it merges with a roadway. 50 metres ahead of the road you go left and, beneath olive trees, finally reach the church **Panagía Palatianí** (**P3:** N36°44.052′/ E26°57.500′, 130 m)

0.30

> *The upper chapel is the successor of the church lower down, which is now in ruins and in whose walls ancient architectural components can be found everywhere. These "spoils" come from the temple to Dionysos which was originally located here.*

On the far side of the hill ③, five metres before reaching the road, you descend left down the field track and, with a panoramic view, pass two farmhouses (left) and bear right *uphill* at the indistinct fork through a farmyard whose chaotic disorder may surprise some people. Further up, walk along the road for 30 m to the right, then, at the next fork, straight on for 100 m, where you find a fence with an **entry** on the right.

!!

0.45

> *On the right, above the entry, you can find traces of the pedestal and a few column drums of a **temple to Demeter.** A seated statue now exhibited in the archaeological museum in Kós was excavated here.*
>
> *Further down, round steps used as seats have been built harmoniously into the slope. These are the remains of the Hellenistic **theatre of Palátia** from the 2nd century BC. The lovely view of the bay enjoyed by the early theatre-goers is now unfortunately almost completely overgrown.*

Back at the fork again, now walk along the road to the right down and turn off it, again to the right, after about 100m. Pass the new house on the left. At the fork to the right of the fence you stroll straight ahead down into a gentle landscape, dominated by a phalanx of wind turbines. Individual pumice-stone boulders rise up from the agricultural valley. At the three right turn-offs you proceed straight ahead until you come to a **house** standing alone in a fenced field on the right (**P4**: N36°43.818'/ E26°56.653').

1.05 Opposite it, a field track turns off at right angles to the left. Wander downhill along it on the left edge of an olive grove until you reach **three cornfield terraces**, spread out in front of you like clover leaves. From the lowest terrace a path runs into a small pine wood (**P5**: N36°43.752'/ E26°56.557'). The path goes through a hollow and then crosses a roadway, where you descend 200m to the right to the large fig trees. (Going to the right from there takes you to a lovely picnic spot next to the ruins of a house.) From the fig trees you proceed left up to the **road** and

1.15 turn off to the right. You saunter downhill on asphalt to the **chapel of Anastásia**.

1.30 Directly in front of it you take the field track down to the left, come through a gate and should be careful not to meddle with a long row of beehives on the left. The roadway continues downhill, makes a sharp left turn and then leads right into the **valley floor** (**P6**: N36°43.123'/ E26°

1.35 56.105'). Further up the valley are the concealed ruins of water mills; a broad roadway runs to the right. Crossing its widened end, you discover, exactly on the far side, a little path through the pine trees. Emerging out of the wood again, you see the valley on the right. At a fork beside a fence you go right, then immediately through a gate and later on to a **barn**. A field track begins there. Go

1.45 right where this joins a wide sand track. The track divides after about 400 m, where you go left down to the beach beside **Áyios Ioánnis Theólogos** ④. Enjoying tremendous

2.05 views, you proceed above the shoreline to the **taverna**.

2.15 Take a nice breather on the terrace and wait for the sun-

ɔW set. Unlike those who have come by car, you have really earned this break!

The way back: You reach the ridge on foot in 50 minutes and need another 30 minutes down to Kamári (see map).

㉗ Sandpipers

On this three-and-a-half hour trek across sand and along country lanes you twice cross the 1.5 km wide isthmus of Kós. It is called "Lavi" ("handle") and has two very different sandy beaches. The beach tavernas are only open in summer.

■ *9 km, difference in altitude 45 m, easy*

AWT	
0.00	From the **bus stop "Paradise Beach"** you trot the first few metres towards the sea on asphalt, turn left at the fork
0.10	and down serpentine bends to **Paradise Beach.**

There you wander left along the strip of sand which later becomes wider ①. The next stretch is known as Landakes- or Banana Beach. Then comes **Markos Beach** with a ta-
0.25 verna. Care for a frappé with a view across the most beautiful beaches on Kós? (Rambling along these, you could reach Kardámena in five hours.)

0.35 From the taverna an ascending road leads us to the **main road.** The roadway continues on the far side, left – in front of a villa. Without turning off it, we traverse a ridge (45 m) and descend as far as a crossroads (**P1:** N36° 46.217′/
0.50 E27°00.708′). Here we first go right and, after 150 m, **left** and down. Leaving the farmhouse to our left, we rush towards the sea between juniper and mastic bushes. After seven minutes we go straight ahead at the fork we come to further down and, at the next one, right to the **beach.**

1.05 Even in high season **Hohylaríou Bay** ② is hardly fre-
★ quented. Here we continue left across the sand. Later arri-
1.20 ving at a **beach kiosk** operated in season, we ascend a driveway 50 m beyond it.

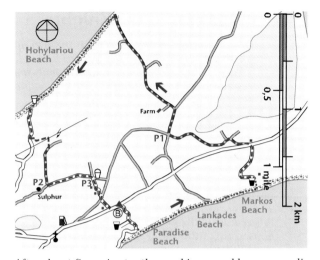

After about five minutes the road is crossed by a power line. Already *100 m before* that we head left down a fairly
wide branch-off and, *after 10 m,* enter a narrow trail on
the right. This leads us along the left side of a cornfield. At
the end of this field – still *ahead of* a wooden electricity
mast – we turn off right at right angles. On the left is now
a potato patch and on the right is still the cornfield. Walking straight ahead to a roadway, continue right along it.

1.35 Further up it joins a transverse, wider **lane**, which we take
to the left. (A hundred meters to the right it is possible to
discover something special: volcanic rocks which emit a
sulphurous odour. They only protrude about half a meter
out of the alluvial land which, geologically speaking, "later" surrounded them. (**P2:** N36°45.899'/ E26°59.822').

The wider lane, which we have taken to the left, is later li-
1.40 ned by reeds on the right. In front of a raised **well** (**P3:**
N36°46.013'/ E27°00.191') it meets a transverse path,
which we take to the right.

Having walked alongside a farmhouse (right), we meet
another transverse path. Going right along it, we take, after 30 m, the short roadway left to the main road. Procee-
1.50 ding left along it for 80 m, we again reach the **little bus
shelter** or hire car.

!! (left margin, line 2)
!! (left margin, line 5)

㉘ The Fortress of the Knights

This three-hour circular tour leads through the impressive eroded valleys in the western half of Kos, which is characterised by its pumice stone, to the gigantic citadel of Andimáchia, which dominates the coastal plain.

■ *8 km, difference in altitude 145 m, easy*

AWT
0.00
0.05

From the taxi rank in **Kardámena** you march up the side street past Louis' supermarket (right). At the top you turn off to the right and come to the **Starlight Club.** Behind it you go up left and past two left turn-offs. You walk up the next one, a double left turn (**P1:** N36°47.251'/ E27° 08.405'). First left, then right you see terraced housing. Proceeding on the field track, you then notice a tall warehouse and, to the left of it, a chapel – your first destination. Walking along the edge of the slope, you reach a

0.15
sheet-metal hut.

There you go through a gate and, without a path, follow the edge of a field and an olive grove as far as the chapel

0.20
and the road. 100 m further to the left stands a **sign** from the European Leader Programme, which helped finance the path leading up the hill. Walk uphill in serpentines ①

0.45
almost to the **citadel's** artificial trench ② (145 m).

The fortress was built under Venetian rule in the 13th century. After 1309 it was so well fortified by the Order of Saint John that an Ottoman siege in 1457 could be repelled by just 15 knights and 300 inhabitants. After the fall of Rhodes in 1523, an honourable withdrawal from Kós was granted to the Order.

Only the defence walls are still standing; the buildings within them are all in ruins following two earthquakes 90 years ago.

Walk 100 m away from the fortress on the approach road and then right, down into an eroded valley on a beautifully curved field track. Down in the plains, go right for a while along a field track which comes from the left and, 1.05   20m after the **concreted ford**, walk right again onto a tractor track. Partly accompanied by a pipe, it follows the valley floor as far as a farmstead (**P2: N36°47.783'/ E27° 08.243'**). 1.15   08.243'). Leave the farm on your left and take the **field track** up to the right You have to circumvent the cheeky fence surrounding a house by going round to the left. Behind it the now indistinct field track leads back to the tall 1.25   **warehouse** on the road. Walk left down it for five minutes before turning right into another road. Beyond two large boat sheds comes a terrace house on the right. Opposite it a well-beaten track drops down across a little 1.40   road to a pool on the **main road** in Kardámena.

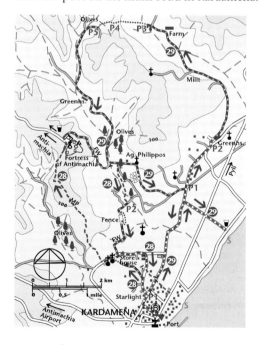

㉙ Arizona

The impressive four-hour circular tour leads from Kardámena through two unspoiled valleys which, with their bizarre rock formations, are reminiscent of Arizona. While there is nowhere to stop off or draw water, the route largely follows country lanes and, for a quarter of an hour, is without a path, but orientation is not a problem.
A short cut could be made by driving to AWT 0.25/P1 with a hire car or taxi.
■ *19 km, difference in altitude 100 m, moderate*

▷ *Map see previous page.*

AWT 0.00	From the taxi stand in the traffic hub of **Kardámena** you take the gently ascending Odos Thymatou to the left of the **department store** "Louis", bearing right at the top.
0.05	A little street lined with eucalyptus trees leads us out of the village past the **"Starlight Club"** (left). Straight ahead
0.15	at the crossing beside the **cemetery** (left), and shortly afterwards going through a rift, we head for the mountains.
0.25	We **cross** a street which runs obliquely – this is where hire car users could park their car (**P1**: N36°47.904'/ E27° 08.749').
0.35	A little further on we see a chapel in the landscape on the left and several buildings on the roadside. At the **road junction** in front of a fence (**P2**: N36°48.280'/ E27° 09.057') we turn left. Shortly after, at a large greenhouse (right), we leave the asphalt and turn off right into a country lane. It too runs towards the mountains, later as-

0.45	cending slightly. From the **ridge of hills** it is possible to see into the next valley, which is framed by cliffs in the background. A picture like in a Western.
0.50	We descend, ignoring a left turn beside the **bunkers** which leads up to a chapel. Having passed a large farmhouse (right), we see a solitary shed 200 m further on ①,
1.00	which we reach by following the ruts **branching left.** A little later we traverse a rift (**P3:** N36°49.188′/ E27° 08.476′). On the right above another rift we climb slowly without a path in the direction of the range of hills. Instead of entering a grey sandy furrow in the terrain, we
1.10	climb left a little more steeply as far as the **saddle** (**P4:** N36°49.204′/ E27°08.113′, 105 m). Enjoying a picnic there, we can gaze down into the green valley and make out the Turkish peninsula Resadyie in the distance.
	On the other side, still without a path, we head towards an olive plantation, but walk left through a rift 100 m before it and then in the direction of the left edge of the
1.15	plantation. In this way we reach a **roadway** (**P5:** N36° 49.198′/ E27°07.953′), descend right and then out of the valley. 200 m beyond a cattle trough, from a hilltop up on the edge of the valley, we catch sight of Andimáchia
1.30	fortress ②. Turning sharp left at a **fork**, we walk past enormous greenhouses (right). Later, shortly after where a
1.50	roadway joins from the right, we traverse a **concrete weir.** This is the point/AWT 1.05 on walk 28. Those of us who wish to make straight for Kardámena follow the description on page 107 from here.
	Those wishing to return to their hire car, or to hop into the water after all, go straight uphill here – first past the Philippos Chapel (left), then past a dilapidated windmill (right). Later, at a cattle trough (left) straight on as far as
2.05	the "oblique" **crossing (P1)**, where the hire car is waiting. Or go right from there and along the first street on the left towards the sea.

㉚ The Turtles in Paléo Pilí

If you don't meet up with a turtle on this four to five-hour walking tour, then you haven't paid attention. Many of these slow-moving animals are at home on the plateau. We are a little faster on our feet, also scale the ruins of a castle and drop in to the ghost village of Paléo Pilí. However, orientation on the paths is not always easy. Apart from a few inns in Amanioú there are two springs along the way.

■ *7 km, difference in altitude 235 m, moderate*

AWT Having arrived in the upper part of **Pilí** (Áyios Nikolaos, 85m) by bus, you can fill your water bottle at the 500-year-old fountain, 100 m outside the village, which has managed to keep its quaintness very well. From the

0.00 **platía**, the square, you walk uphill along the street lead-

0.04 ing to Kardámena. After 300 m, follow the **sign** to the "Heroon of Charmylos" to the left, and walk *straight* on at

0.07 the **second sign**.

> *The detour left down to the so-called **grave of Charmylos**, a mythological hero, is not exactly a "must". The sober barrel vaults, each with six lateral recesses for graves, were built upon many times, the last time with a chapel whose walls contain ancient building components from the former constructions.*

!! From the "second sign" you go downhill and, *two metres before* the fork in the road further down ① (**P1: N36°50.491'/ E27°09.801'**), right onto a well-beaten track

0.10 running alongside a **gully** and, after 30m, uphill. In open country you veer left along a well-beaten track to a wide

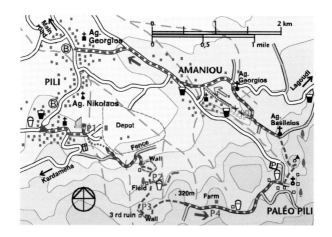

roadway, which you should follow steeply upwards to the
0.15 right. From the round **hilltop** you can see – 200 m as the
crow flies – the ruins of a house on the next hill – your
first goal. Down on the left is a military depot, which ex-
plains why the spot is not really suitable for taking holiday photos.

Descending into the hollow, you go about 60 m to the left
0.20 on the **roadway** at the bottom. Taking a roadway that
forks to the right, you come up to the dilapidated house.
Behind it is a flat field. Next to the stump of an olive tree
0.25 on the right is a **passageway** (**P2:** N36°50.310'/ E27°
10.225') through the wall. This is where a footpath lined
with bushes and kermes oaks begins to lead uphill to the
0.30 **second ruin** ② with a few olive trees. Leaving this on
your right, you take a right turn, on the left of the wall, on
0.40 up through rocky terrain to a plateau with a **third ruin**
(**P3:** N36°50.070'/ E27°10.112', 255 m). This remains 50 m
to the right of your route, which initially runs left beside a
meadow and later, in front of the boulders, makes a wide
curve to the left ③. Soon you will find a convenient goat
path. Up on the right the chapel of Saint George reveals
itself briefly in a groove in the terrain. In the sea you can
make out Kálymnos and, further to the right, Psérimos,
while along the coast of Kos you see the former saltworks,
which is now a bird sanctuary. The mountain with the antennas is dedicated to the prophet Elijah.

0.45	At the top you meet up with a **field track** (320 m), which
1.00	you follow to the left. Past a **farmstead** (left) (**P4: N36°** 50.071'/ E27°10.626') and (probably) a few turtles, you come to a watering-place. The ruins of the old castle can already be spotted . At the fork you proceed straight ahead and then downhill through the remains of the vil-
1.15	lage of **Paléo Pilí** (Old Pilí). The hidden location in the mountains protected the inhabitants from pirates, but not from illness. In 1830 the village was abandoned due to cholera. As you climb up through the remains of the walls, you pass a chapel of St. Mary with neglected frescoes.
1.25	From the Byzantine **castle ruins** from the 12th century you can enjoy the panorama of the northern coast.
!!	As you descend, leave the path to the right *50 m above* the parking area to reach a lovely old paved path leading to
1.35	the **chapel of Áyios Basileios.** A field track below the shady sitting area leads further downhill. Go right at the fork after 100m. A little further on you see a gate on the left. (By going straight on down the roadway from here, it is also possible to reach the road at the bottom near a chapel. This is the easier, but longer route.)
	Behind the aforementioned gate stands a hut; walk to the right of it. A few metres to the left is the old overgrown path, which you use as a guide line, always keeping to the right of it without a path. Passing through olive groves, you come to a roadway. Past a horse ranch (left) you reach
1.55	the road, where you go left to **Amanioú.** Since the terrain on the left is a restricted military area, it is only possible to
2.10	return to **Pilí** along the road (lower part of the town called Áyios Geórgios).

③ The Peak

This four-hour ascent of Mount Díkeos is a must, even for languid beach tourists. It should be undertaken on a clear day since sudden fog can become a problem. Don't forget to take water!
The moderately steep climb through pine forests is well marked. Those with a fear of heights needn't worry, the only problem being one short passage beneath the peak.

■ *8 km, difference in altitude 560 m, moderate*

AWT   The little village of **Zía** (285 m), beautifully situated in a mountain forest, strikes the new-comer as a disappointment at first since there are rows of shops lined up one next to another. In the upper part, however, there are nice houses and small streets.

0.00   Head up the lane beginning directly beside the nut tree on the right of the **bus stop**, leaving the stalls behind you after a few metres. Passing a water mill (left), you walk across the terrace of an inn to reach the church above. Turn right in front of the church and walk uphill. Bear right again at the fork and follow the "Way to the Mountain" up to the left, past the witty taverna "Zia" (right). Later blue dots accompany you up the cement street.

0.10   Immediately after a house with a large porch (right), turn up right onto a **cement street**, where you will soon appreciate the pleasant shade of the pine trees. 50 m after a

0.15   chapel (right) ①, in the bend, go through a **gate** on the left. Walk uphill to the right behind the fence, staying on the right. The peak can't be seen yet. On a beautiful old

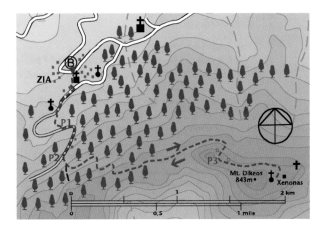

0.20   rocky path you meet up again with the **sandy street** (**P1:** N36°50.353'/ E27°12.117'). Walking left up the street, you

0.25   soon see a small **farmhouse** (left). After another house, stroll on for 300 m enjoying the pine aroma until, before

0.30   a right-hand bend, a red **metal arrow** (**P2:** N36°50.082/ E27°11.885') on the left indicates the beginning of the ascent through the woods.

!!   Bear *left after 50 m* at a fork and follow the serpentine trail through the forest. Back in the open again, after a curve to

1.00   the right and a wind gap, you reach a **foothill** (**P3:** N36° 49,871'/ E27°12,057', 730 m). From here you have a view of the other side of the island and the old fishing harbour of Kardámena, which has completely surrendered to tourism.

Follow the markings to the left, now only slightly ascending to a ridge. With your destination in view, first walk

1.15   downhill and then up to the **summit chapel** ②. This affords splendid views across the gentle north side and the rugged southern coast of Kos, surrounded by many of the Dodecanese islands and the narrow Turkish peninsula of Resadiye. For such a panorama you will gladly make a donation to the chapel by lighting a candle. The inhabitants of Kos love to celebrate up here. A xenonas, a guesthouse, offers overnight accommodation and protection from bad weather.

2.25   Take the same route to get back to **Zía**.

㉜ To the Asklepieion

If you haven't overburdened yourself at the souvenir shops in Zía, you can wander down to the famous excavations of the Asklepieion along roadways with breathtaking views in five hours. You pass through two abandoned villages, but will find no wells.
■ *13 km, difference in alt. 270 m, moderate to difficult*

AWT 0.00	At the end of **Zía's** shopping mile, walk out of the village past the **taverna "Ayli"** (left). After 400 m under pine trees pass the bus parking area on the left and turn off to
!!	the right onto the road. 250 m further on, *100 m ahead of the turn-off,* wander down into the valley on the left until
0.07 0.10	you come to a small **stone bridge** (**P1:** N36°50.898'/ E27°12.289'), where you take the pathway to **Asómatos**, a part of the village of Asfendíou. It is decaying and has almost been abandoned – it is simply easier to earn money on the coast. Individual houses have been restored by foreigners. On the left of the church to Saint George, you come to some stone steps leading uphill and, staying
0.15	slightly on the right, arrive at the **road** again, where you go left. On the next elevation you go straight ahead at a crossing below the cemetery (right).

The road continues almost on the same level and affords a fine view over olive groves and the sea. Disregard the left turn-off of a field track, but then, after about eight minutes, you must be careful not to miss the **footpath** (**P2:** N36°51.172'/ E27°13.654') *leading downhill to the left.* It starts beside a culvert and becomes narrower further down due to a large boulder.

Here it is possible to descend into the ghost village of **Áyios Dimítrios** in five minutes. The church is closed, only permitting a glimpse of the interior with its old wall paintings from the vestibule.

0.35   If you stay on the now sloping road, a wide **sand track** leads up right after four minutes, beyond a culvert in a sharp left-hand bend.

> *Alternative:* The Asklepieion can also be reached on the asphalt road in an AWT of just 1.25 hours.

0.45
0.50   Ignoring the track that turns off to the right a little later, go left on the same level at the following fork. 200 m later you traverse a **gully** before you zigzag your way up through a pine forest to a wide **roadway** and look down on the town of Kós (**P3:** N36°51.231'/ E27°14.400').

Here you go left, stay in the right-hand bend and drop down towards an agricultural enterprise. Before reaching it, you walk up right at a crossing to visit the tiny grotto chapel Panagía Melóu ⬛. From there you descend, without a path, to the roadway which runs below it, turn right and then go uphill. On the first elevation are giant plane trees, then the smell of sulphur reminds one how thin the earth's crust is on Kos. Yellowish water bubbles up out of the ground. You climb up through empty, wild countryside. On the wayside you come across a spring and deserted chapel (**P4:** N36°

1.20   51.361'/ E27°15.243'). Having passed a prominent **rock** (left, 335 m) and a solitary tree on the wayside, the surroundings become more hospitable again and you can make out the Turkish peninsula of Bodrum. Taking a right-hand curve ②, you go round a hill until you see several tubes lying on the path: up to the right a spring beneath trees has supplied water since time immemorial (**P5:** N36°51.489'/ E27°15.724').

Beside the tubes you leave the roadway at right angles to your direction of movement, dropping down to the left. In the gully below commences the most strenuous part of the trek. First you go through a gate fastened with knots and descend into a hollow. In front of the fence above the military shelters you bear right and go through a wide gate.

Walking along the right-hand side of the following fence, set your bearings on the rocky hill. First comes another fence: In front of it descend to the right as far as an opening in the fence or even further to the wide gate (**P6:** N36°51.729'/ E27°15.664'), also fastened with ornate knots, which stands immediately below a rocky outcrop. After retieing the gate, you take in a left-hand curve round

1.45 the hill without a path until you cross the **roadway** which runs downhill. There's no stopping you now: down you go, past a small farmstead standing up to your left.

In front of the pine forest further down you go right onto

2.00 the transversal **field track.** Later you can shorten a wide curve by climbing down to the left cross-country. At the fork down on the level you go right, later walking left

2.10 across the field to the car park of the **Asklepieion** (**P7:** N36°52.593'/ E27°15.521').

> *This "spa sanatorium" was dedicated to Asklepios (in Latin: Aesculapius), Apollo's son and the god of healing. More than 300 shrines to Asklepios are said to have existed in Greece; this was the most important one. Even the location is magnificent, although the view of the mainland is now almost completely overgrown. It was constructed from the 3rd century BC and then expanded in the Hellenistic and Roman periods. In an exciting crescendo the site was dominated by a temple on the highest of the three terraces. The altar, the oldest building, was located on the middle terrace, with hallways forming the reception area on the lowest terrace.*
>
> *Having been destroyed by an earthquake, the sanctuary was long forgotten and it was not until 100 years ago that it was excavated by the German archaeologist Rudolf Herzog.*

From here, there is a little trolley-train back to town.

Chálki

The entry into the harbour offers one of the most beautiful scenes in all of Greece. The respectable merchants' houses have been restored with loving care and offer lodging for visitors. They are preferably leased directly to guests from the UK. The island counts on a more distinguished and quieter kind of mature tourist. Private accommodation is very scarce. For hiking on the rather barren island it is best to buy a map from the publishers Anavasi.

33 The Green Side

Judging by the arid landscape above picturesque Empório it is hard to imagine that the island also has green areas. Some of them will be discovered on this tour – in a side valley and on the island's far side.
To get there, it takes two-and-a-half hours, a bottle of water, food and bathing things.
■ *5 km, difference in alt. 125 m, easy to moderate*

AWT 0.00   Soaring above the north side of **Empório** harbour is the filigree tower of **St. Nicholas church.** At the rear exit from the churchyard with its wonderful pebble surface, hop sprightly up the four steps, walk to the right along the alley and bear left at the fork, then left again. Pass the "Captain's House" pension and cross the street. Up at the edge of the village, on the far right, you later see a dilapidated two-storey house, which you can reach by taking small detours.

0.05 On the right of these ruins, a **gate** reveals a monopáti ① leading uphill to the left of a wall into stony nature. After a right curve, head towards the ruins of the Kyriakí chapel, but turn off uphill to the left 250 m before it, where the wall ends on the right. On the left here is a half-high

0.10 **cistern.** Striding over a saddle, cross a **country lane** and
0.15 walk down through an olive grove to reach the **concrete**
0.20 **road** behind it.

Walk comfortably downhill along the street for 300 m until just before a thick pine forest. Skilfully open the

0.25 **double gate** beside the cistern on the left of the road and follow the lane, with the trees on your right. As you walk,

0.30 look for a cave up on the slope ②. At the end of the **left curve** (**P1:** N 36°14.027′/ E 27°36.789′), leave the lane to the right, climb uphill over stone terraces, always towards

0.35 the cave, below which you walk through a risky **passageway** made of an old spring mattress frame and then turn right.

For 70 metres the way is almost flat, and then in front of the barricade you go up left into the rocks along a narrow

0.45 marked path. Up on the **saddle** (125 m) are abandoned fields whose cultivation hasn't been worthwhile for some time now, yet in Antiquity a temple stood here. As you continue your way, you see juniper bushes down below.

0.50 This lovely green region is called **"Pefkia"**, which means pines. There aren't many of them left, however, although it rains more often up here.

Return by the same path, but turn off downhill to the left

1.05 after the **mattress door.** Then you must imitate the goats and descend across the terraces in the fields to the road

1.20 and the **beach at Kaniá.** "Beach" is a bit exaggerated, but it is good enough for a quick swim.

25 m before the petrol station for boats, walk along a concrete track to the right at the edge of the sea

1.25 to arrive at the **fish farm.**

Here you can see how the problem of the overfishing of the Mediterra-nean is going to be solved: fish spawn along with feed is brought over from Italy, fed to become bream and then, for the most part, sent back again.

About 40 m before the hall, take a footpath to the right, go round the installation between pointed rocks, pass through a gate and then walk directly along the seaside for another little bit. After a low cliff, turn uphill to the

1.40 right to reach a narrow trekking path into a **saddle.** Up there you should, for a start, enjoy the beautiful panorama of the harbour with the Kastro hill. After that you are

1.50 soon in **Empório** and can choose a nice table at the harbour. Read the menu with special interest today. Does it offer bream?

㉞ Faded Frescoes

This six to seven-hour, partly marked hike leads to two medieval fortified settlements. You can see abandoned villages, the ruins of a castle and faded frescoes in ancient chapels.
■ *13 km, difference in altitude 445 m, difficult*

AWT 0.00	At the **jetty in Empório**, walk up the street, past the school and then along the "Blvd. Tarpon Spring" (a place in Florida to which many local sponge divers emigrated)
0.10	as far as **Póndamos** beach. Beyond it, the street ascends and demands a certain amount of energy. The island taxi will pass you several times. Don't show any signs of weakness now! In front of you are the first destinations: up on the left, the castle, and then the cloister of Taxiárchis amidst gardens on the mountain on the right.
0.20 0.25	Standing on the left of the way is a **chapel** and later a roadside cross. 100 m after this cross, open the **gate** up on the left and follow the gravelly path directly above the
0.40	fence. It ends at a **doorway** on the street. Go up the street for two curves until, after four minutes, you find a foot-
0.50	path leading up left to **Chorió**. The village was deserted after the war, but recently some houses have been restored by expatriate Greeks.

If you want to enjoy the magnificent view from the ruins of the castle, first walk up to the larger church, then go through the door on the right in the churchyard and go up left along the steep path. Halfway up, opposite the entry to a small barrel-vaulted chapel, you clearly recognise the square hewn stones of the Hellenic acropolis which

dominated the hill long before the castle of the Order of St. John. The St. Mary chapel is also very old (890 AD, restored in 1971) and is decorated with frescoes inside.

1.05 You enter the the14th century **castle** through the tower keep, which is enclosed on all sides and hence easily defensible. In the castle church completely unprotected frescoes await a better future. The most rewarding thing about the castle, though, is the distant view across the sea.

1.15 When you are back down on the **road**, take the old path on the left of the cemetery walls (incorporating ancient components), through a gate and ascend below the road until – on the paved road – you come past an interesting

1.25 **grotto chapel** in the saddle (255 m). Directly after the rock, a concrete path on the right leads down to the church of **Áyios Leftérios.** Behind the larger, white church, you find a hidden ancient little church with old images whose faces were probably disfigured with scratches in the Islamic period. To prevent complete ruin, they have at least now been protected by gauze.

Behind the church the markings first point through the
!! fence, then *up left,* through another fence and round a
1.45 right curve to the **Moní Taxiárchis** (310 m), the cloister of the archangels, called "San Angela" in the Italian period. Here, too, the most interesting church is the smaller one with its frescoes. But most of all the epicure on this side of eternity enjoys the wonderful picnic spot ⬚ up here and the view over to Rhodes.

Having enjoyed all this, wander west along the flat con-
1.55 crete track until you come to the **road**, where you turn up to the right. (Turning back here saves two hours.) After twelve minutes you see a gap in the fence on the right – for later! The slowly ascending, oversized road is a bit discouraging, but you are rewarded for your efforts with the view into the charming high valley with its fields enclosed by stone walls.

In the saddle (440 m), on the right below Profitis Elias, is
2.15 the **torso of a windmill** and a small field chapel. The asphalt street continues to the cloister of Áyios Ioánnou. But you should take the lane to the right leading to the deserted settlement of **Kílla.** It is of Hellenistic origin and later was an outside village for the goatherds from Chorió, abandoned after the Turkish period. Besides Hellenistic

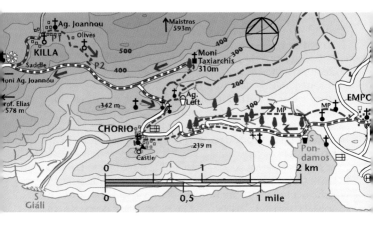

building remains it is also possible to find the remains of frescoes in the dilapidated church apse of square hewn stones. As you walk around between the ruins with the wind whistling in your ears, you are quickly seized by a sense of the finiteness of mortal life, increased even more by the putrid smell from the dragon arum blossoms. Un-

2.25 fortunately, the more recent church, **Áyios Ioánniou** (**P1**: N36°13.853′/ 27°34.526′) ☑, located on a dreamlike terrace, is locked up.

Go back through the hollow covered with olive trees, with the glistening sea visible beyond. If you expect to admire more faded frescoes in the next dilapidated chapel along the way, you will be disappointed – only the goats you disturb will jump out. The old path to the sea is easier

2.40 to find from up above, and you soon arrive at the **road** below (**P2**: N36°13.663′/ 27°34.710′); go left down it.

!! Below Chorió – after a right-hand bend – you find *blue-red markings on the left* indicating a path which runs along the valley bottom past an oil press and ends at the beach

3.45 of **Póndamos.** You only have two choices to make here: swimming or Nick's taverna.

▷ The "Captain's House" (tel. 22460-45201) and the "Kleánthi" (tel. 22460-45334) offer **overnight accommodation.**

Kássos

Although Kássos is only four kilometres from Kárpathos, it is rarely frequented by foreign visitors. The sterile, over-sized harbour gives no reason to expect an idyllic island. This aspect can rather be found in the neighbouring old fishing harbour Boúka and the former landing stage in Emborió. In addition, you will meet especially friendly people living on the island, and they will soon make you feel at home. But the choice of places to stay is limited.

The landscape is almost devoid of trees and fairly barren, as it only has a few springs. Although many paths are now asphalted, some monopátia and narrow country lanes can still be discovered for hiking. The wind is extremely strong in the mountains and almost takes your breath away at times.

㉟ The Massacre of Kássos

This easy circular tour takes four hours and leads to an ancient shrine in a cave and to the extensive northern coast with a chapel on the beach. The trek starts and finishes on little used roads. Refreshments are only available in Ayía Marína.
■ *12 km, difference in alt. 110 m, easy to moderate*

AWT From the small, picturesque fishing harbour **Boúka** ④,
0.00 take the street leading up into the village, with the town hall and antenna on your right, and turn off left onto the side-street and bear right where it forks. Later walk re-
0.05 spectfully on the right of the two **white gentlemen** and on up the right track.

At the narrow street's turn-off to the right, continue straight on along the old footpath leading uphill alongside the **cemetery.** Later a narrow lane passes on the right of a church and leads into the village of **Ayía Marína.** Continue uphill to arrive at the **outdoor café** at the top (still before the second large church) and walk along the larger street downhill to the left. Circle round an olive grove (left) in a wide left curve to come to a nicely restored windmill (left) in the Kathistres district. At the traffic sign shortly after it, walk to the right. Soon you will arrive at the **Fanoúrius Church** on the right with the torso of a windmill opposite it.

0.10

0.20

0.30

After 50 m, walk downhill slightly and then straight ahead at two turn-offs to the right. The **concrete ends,** and you continue straight on along the sand, with the sea on the right and two paths in front of you ①: the new flagstone path on the left leading uphill to the cave and the other one going further right to the sea.

0.35

Along a curiously curved, elaborate flagstone path (with lighting!) you reach the entrance door. If it is locked, you might have to clamber over the wall further up in order to reach the mouth of the cave ② (**P1:** N35°24.165'/ E26°54.241').

0.45

*The **cave of Ellinikokamára** was always a hiding-place and cult site. The Dorians closed off the side facing the sea with enormous square hewn stones. The view of the sea is actually more rewarding.*

Take the same way back and then go sharply to the left at the bottom. A narrow cart track leads to a **goat pen** in a gully in the terrain, where you pass a gate. The way becomes a path which soon leads past the **grotto chapel**

0.55

1.00

Áyios Mínas (right). This subterranean room is also very impressive, in spite of being much smaller than the cave. Behind the newly laid out garden an indistinct path leads on the left of the fence. After two further gullies it runs above walled terraces (**P2:** N35°24.028'/ E26°53.825'; 80 m).

1.10 In the next gully you see two little **pump houses** up on the left as well as the end of the power line.

Soon afterwards comes another roadway, which leads you slightly downhill; ignore the two left turn-offs. Enjoy the extensive panorama of the coast, watched over by a

!! chapel ③. After a gate *before* a gully, meander down to the

1.25 **sea** along serpentine curves. Wide pebble beaches await you, and you have really earned them.

> *The **monument** at the car park commemorates the darkest period in the island's history. In 1824, during the Greek war for independence, Egyptian troops landed here and caused a terrible bloodbath, killing 1000 people. The survivors were enslaved and removed to what was then the Ottoman Egypt. A few of them could return after 10 years, while other descendants returned in the 1950s.*

Once you have thoroughly enjoyed the beaches, wander

1.40 along the street to the chapel of **Áyios Konstantinos.** Utensils for the church anniversary festival can be found on the dais and in the annex. From here, stroll along the asphalt past the airport to reach the fishing harbour Boú-

2.25 ka in **Fry** once again ④.

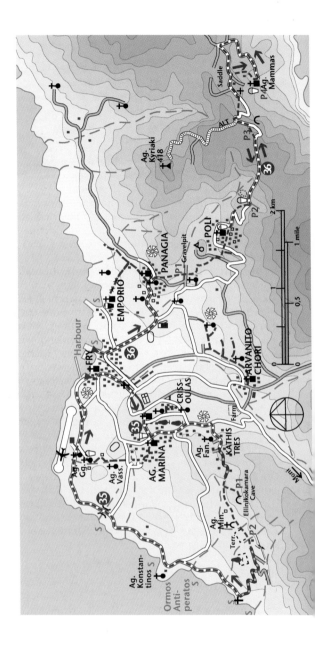

㊱ The Heavenly Convent

Situated above the steep coast on the southern side of the island is an abandoned convent. It used only to be reachable along trails. A large white cross on the mountain ridge showed the pilgrim the way. The five-hour walk described here leads to this beautiful spot above the sea, avoiding the new road that leads there whenever possible. The ascent can be strenuous in hot weather, but the distant views of the sea certainly make up for it. Water can be found at the church in Póli and in the convent itself. Food should be taken along.

■ *18 km, difference in altitude 420 m, difficult*

▷ *Map see previous page.*

AWT	In **Fry**, you will be happy to turn your back on the enormous harbour and march uphill along the main street to
0.00	
	the petrol station (right), where you turn left towards
0.10	**Panagía.** The way through the lower part of the village is almost flat before you go up to the right in front of a barrel-vaulted chapel. In the middle of the village, walk uphill behind the playground. On the right of the street is
0.15	an unusual building complex – **six chapels** next to one another ⬛. From the front, the little doorplates make it resemble a row of terraced houses – the only difference being that the inhabitants are saints.

After 50 m leave the little street in a right curve and walk straight on to reach a monopáti, a bit overgrown, but leading idyllically along the edge of the plains. It is inter-

0.20   rupted by the **access road** to a gravel pit in the gorge, but its continuation, raised on the other side, is easy to find (**P1**: N35°24.561'/ E26°55.982').

At the next fork, bear left uphill, accompanied by walls on both sides and partly overgrown with mastix bushes. At

0.25   times the path goes along bare rock with **steps** hewn into it ②. These are interrupted by a lane, along which you go right for some metres and then continue uphill. At the fork beneath the village, take the path leading uphill to the left and circumnavigate a fence further up on the left.

0.30   Cross the **road** and walk up to the right on a steep concrete path and get into the maze of houses in **Póli**. This used to be the main village of the island, protected in Antiquity and the Middle Ages by a castle. The Venetian kástro now lies in ruins. But the village has recovered somewhat, after having become almost dilapidated.

Next to the cemetery at the far end of the village, the

0.40   Church of the Holy Trinity, **Ayía Triáda** (180 m), awaits your visit. Its cistern offers a last chance to stock up on water before the ascent begins.

The wide asphalt road leading uphill begins on the right side of the church. Only three minutes later, though, the skillfull hiker leaves it again in the first sharp curve to the right to find a monopáti leading upwards and later to the left. Later there is only a wall on the left and after 100 m the path continues cross-country. Near some walls and an

0.50   old **cistern** beside an olive grove (**P2**: N35°24.046'/ E26° 56.612') you come to the road again, which was laid over the old trail from this point on. Many old terraces in the fields extend down to the valley below. Above them on the left is the summit church, Áyios Kiriakí.

You encircle the valley in a wide curve to the left, but leave the road to the left (arrow) in the first sharp curve to the right. The old **pack-mule trail** (**P3**: N35°24.054'/ E26°56.993') reappears – leading upwards in a short-cut, and then you follow the road to the left again.

1.00

    Alternative: The following **turn-off** to the left leads, in a quarter of an hour, to the **summit chapel, Áyios Kiriakí**, a donation from a London shipping magnate who originally came from Kássos. The chapel offers a magnificent view over to Kárpathos.

About 80 m after this turn-off, you can follow an arrow to the left and shorten the way again. This path is fairly stony, however, and ends up at the **road** again. Ignore a turn-off to the left, and soon you will find yourself on the ridge (420 m), with a house (right). A roaring wind often rages here.

1.10

After the ridge, your next turn-off is the second, more indistinct one to the right. This path leads to a little pump house, where you have a view directly down to the convent situated majestically above the sea ③.

★

1.20

    *The **convent of Áyios Mámmas** (**P4**: N35°23.861'/ E26°57.286', 360 m) is dedicated to the shepherds' saint, who, according to the legend, at the intercession of the nuns, transformed three Turkish pirate ships threatening the convent into the three rocks which now lie down in the sea.*

    Inside the church the iconostasis and the wonderful pebble mosaic floor are particularly impressive. The floor depicts two lions and the Byzantine double-headed eagle. The lovely garden with a good cistern and an eternal view of the sea seem to make the convent float in the heavens. Especially on 1st and 2nd September, the church anniversary festival.

For the way back, it is wise to select the longer, but more comfortable road leading upwards. It offers tremendous views of the rocky coast as far as Kárpathos. At the top, walk to the left at the fork. To the right, you could wander to the end of the island at Aktí.

1.35   Soon you will be back on the **ridge** and begin the descent.

1.55   At the walled olive grove you come to the **cistern** again

2.20   (right) and the short-cut to **Póli** ④. This time it is proba-

2.45   bly more relaxing to walk along the street to **Fry!** Maybe you might run into a helpful driver.

③⑦ The lower villages

The route passes through ordinary farmland and the villages of the coastal plain in four hours, following country lanes and mule tracks as well as, occasionally, roads. The villages became repopulated after the medieval threat of pirates was eliminated and it was possible to leave the secure Polí again.

■ *8 km, difference in altitude 115 m, easy*

AWT 0.00	From the picturesque **fishing harbour** of Boúka in **Fry** you stroll up the coastal road and use a short-cut path to the right shortly before the airfield. Passing the "termi-
0.15	nal", you reach the signposted **left turn** and, via a spring, the Áyios Geórgios Vrísis chapel. On the slope are the remains of a noble residence.

To the right of the church door you climb over the sitting step and come after a few meters onto a fairly large expanse with rock ledges, where you make for the high wall of a ruin. You ascend to the left of a field wall and then right in front of the high wall. In the middle of a wide 0.25 meadow you continue uphill to a **monopáti** (**P1**: N35° 25.042'/ E26°54.523').

You traverse a large expanse on ledges; while doing so, the Vassílis chapel is about 150 m to your right. After a further 0.30 short monopáti you come to a **road** and the village of **Ayía Marína**. Go right there, and again at the next two forks. But in the maze of alleys you then bear left and look 0.40 out for the large **Stavrós Church** (**P2**: N35°24.727'/ E26°54.645'; 110 m).

Directly beside it you may find that the café To Steki

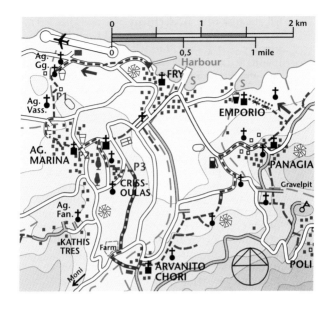

(right) is open. From there the route leads straight ahead, before dropping down to the Ayía Marína Church ☐ and then, in front of it, right. Turn off left immediately after

0.45 another **church** (left) in the Chrissoulas district. First you go straight ahead, later zigzag downhill to a road, where you go down left (on the right further up stands an enclosed church). To the right of the road are olive trees and after 100 m a house whose facade is covered with playful dolphins.

Right in front of it a narrow footpath runs down to a

0.50 **country lane (P3: N35°24.512'/ E26°54.821')**. It leads you right, towards a village, before reaching a road near an ostrich farm. You walk right 150 m up the road and

1.05 then left to the **Church** of **Arvanitochóri**. The name means "village of the Albanians". After the island had become depopulated following the massacre of 1824, the Turkish occupying power settled Albanians here.

Below the church steps you saunter straight on, turn right at a large square with a cistern (left) and pass another, smaller cistern (left). A concrete track leads you past a pretty chapel with forecourt ☐. After 30 m you turn off left at a fork with an electricity pole and later left again into a rocky mule track, which runs downhill rather uncomfortably.

!! It ends at a broad dirt track, 20 m away from the road. *Before* actually reaching the roadway, you go right along the trail running above it through the fields as far as another dirt track. Here you descend left and later right on the

1.25 road. After a **chapel on the roadside** (right) you come to the main road, which you take down to the left.

Just past the petrol station (left) you follow the road on

1.35 the right to **Panagía** and, below the **Hotel Theoxenia**, turn off left. (Further up stands an original "six-pack" chapel, see p. 129).

Below the voluminous village church (right) you wander out of the village along a narrow, level path and, behind a holiday house (left), down to the left. The path is later

1.45 overgrown, so you have to strike out to **Embório** without a path.

In the shallow old harbour it is already possible to bathe in spring. Or savour *dolmádika* – thumb-sized stuffed vine leaves –, the speciality of Kássos is served at the harbour taverna.

Kastellórizo

This tiny island on the eastern edge of Europe is astonishingly cosmopolitan. This may stem from the island's many different masters in the last century: the Turks, the French, the English and the Italians. And also certainly from the forced exodus of the population to Cyprus and Egypt during the last war. In the Golden Twenties, "Castellorizon" served as a landing place for French seaplanes from and to India and had a legendary reputation as Mikró Parísi, Little-Paris.
As the wanderer enters the inviting harbour, his heart skips a beat when he sees the harsh vertical cliffs rising up behind the little town. You can wander comfortably on the plateau, however, although it has neither much shade nor useable cisterns. The few shops offer everything you need for your tour – even a good map of the island for further forays.

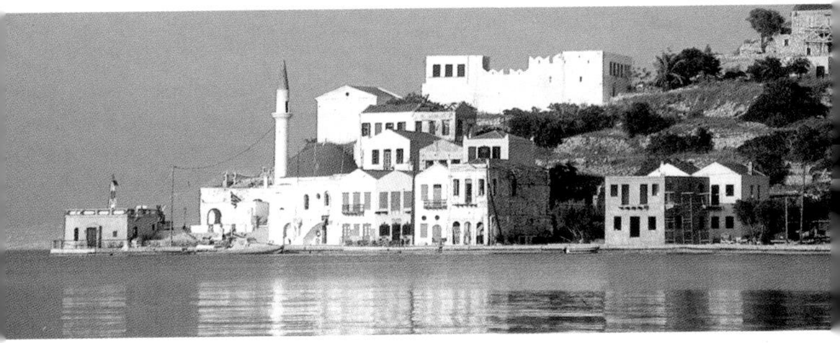

㊳ At the Edge of Europe

This easy walk along the coast takes two and a half hours and leads to a chapel at the edge of Europe. The way back offers a magnificent view of the harbour and the cliffs towering behind it. There are no wells.
■ 4 km, difference in altitude 90 m, easy

AWT 0.00 At the **harbour**, leave the boats bobbing on the right and walk north. At the playground, you go up left and then right on the flagstone path. Next to the antenna mast, 30 m

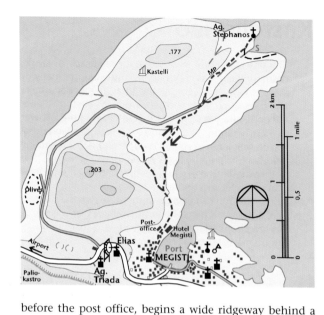

before the post office, begins a wide ridgeway behind a gate. It leads through an olive grove, with a lovely view of the offshore islands, and then continues above the coast. On the hilltop a roadway approaches on the left. Walk for about five minutes parallel to it on the right on a path which finally merges with the roadway. Soon afterwards the roadway ends and you can use the old **path** to reach, without any orientation problems, the little church of **Saint Stephan.**

0.30

0.40

It is situated on the top of a cliff, like an outpost of Christianity facing the Asian continent. The Greek military use this spot, too, so that the Turks won't take them by surprise, but the inhabitants of Kastellórizo enjoy shopping in Kas, the Turkish village facing them.

At the creek you can get into the water from the flat rocks. Return along the same lovely path you came on, with a beautiful view of **Megísti.**

1.20

▷ **Pension** Caretta (tel: 02460-49208) has tastefully furnished rooms.

㊴ Patitíria – Ancient Winepresses

In ancient times, Megísti (its former name, which meant "the greatest") was at least great in viticulture. Cavities cut into the cliffs for pressing wine are still preserved. You will find some of these, visit a decaying fortified monastery and climb up the Dorian acropolis. To accomplish all this, you need three to four hours and a lot of water. Before setting off, you can try to get the key to the St. George's monastery from the priest (papas) down in the village.

■ *5 km, difference in altitude 250 m, moderate*

AWT
0.00

★

0.15

0.25

At the top of the village, on the right next to the little spire of the **church** of St. George *(of the field)*, you proceed vigorously up the street and then ascend a stone stairway opposite the junction ①. A magnificent path of steps (picture on rear book cover) leads slowly up through the rocks. From here, you look out to sea and over to the Turkish city of Kas. The steps end at the **plateau** (165 m). You can easily find the red-coloured path to the south here, up on the left of a fenced field. Walk to the left in front of the fortified monastery ②. Directly next to the path, on the left in the rocks, is a horizontal shaft with an antechamber – an ancient grave now used as a goat pen.

The fortified monastery Áyios Geórgios tou Bonioú (Saint George of the Mountain), built in 1790, has been abandoned and is slowly decaying. Take great care when entering. Through a gap in the wall, you can see the courtyard with its windows shaped like gun slits and the free-standing church, the katholikón. If you have the key,

you can see the icons of St. George on the iconostasis in the church, on the far left next to the Virgin Mary.

An exciting entry into a dark, narrow opening leads down to a grotto crypt dedicated to Saint Charálampos, "The Radiant". Salutary water drips from the walls.

60 to 70 m south of the monastery, behind a fenced field, is another sight worth seeing: a "patitíri", an ancient winepress ③.

At least three circular cavities were cut Into large, almost flat rocks. One hollow had no drain, and two were connected by a groove. Archaeologists explain their function as follows: first the grapes were placed in the hollow without a drain, where they were pressed to a certain extent by their own weight. A very sweet wine was produced from this juice. Then the grapes were pressed in wooden rings in the upper hollow by stamping feet, the mash trickling into the lower hollow and gathering there. So far 47 such patitíria have been found on the island.

Our way leads down from the monastery without a path to the large square cistern (**P1:** N36°08.474'/ 29°35.385') behind the eucalyptus tree in the dip and from there to the right, onto the shady field. After the pines swing to
0.30 the left in *front of a **house***, over a stone wall and onto a distinct path to the right. At the intersection with a trans-
0.35 versal **path** (**P2:** N36°08.739'/ E29°35.309'), turn left. Be-
0.40 hind a water trough, go right as far as the **Cyclopean Wall**, directly above where the slope falls away.

Cyclopean walls are enormous dry stones layered on top of one another without continuous horizontal joints. This one comes from the Mycenaean Era (1500 to 1300 BC) and extended the natural cliff wall to the rift.

Short Cut: From here you can go downhill to reach Ayía Triáda monastery in eight minutes.

A slightly rising mule track directly next to the wall leads inland on the right of a rift, past a farmstead (right), to
0.50 the (locked) church of **Áyios Ioánnis.**

Shortly before it, directly along the monastery's fence on the right of the path, you discover another, even more nicely executed patitíri. (The second one in this area is very difficult to find.)

The path goes uphill on the right of the old solitary olive tree. Hard to find at first, it becomes broader later on and
0.55 leads safely up to the **country lane.** Walking along this

1.00   up to the right, you come to the **saddle** (235 m), keenly watched by the soldiers on Mount Vígla. A footpath leads downhill exactly opposite the junction, on the right of the walled Saint Panteleimos church and up to the

1.10   **Paleókastro** (250 m) ④.

> *This place has been fortified since very early times. In the Hellenic Age gigantic square hewn stones were assembled to form the massive walls of a city, which was dedicated to Apollo. In Byzantine times, and under the Order of St. John, rough stone walls were laid on top of them. The Italians used cement for the foundations of their gun positions. The three chapels form a peaceful contrast to the militaristic surroundings.*
>
> *The many, sometimes immense, cisterns with a smooth finish on the inside are fascinating. Thirst was certainly the most dangerous enemy of the citadel's inhabitants.*

Our wondrous gaze pans across the mountains in Asia Minor and the many islets in front of them. In the west lies the larger island of Ro, where, completely alone, the country woman Déspina stood her ground for Greece from 1927 to 1962 by chasing away Turkish invaders. There is a monument to her at the beginning of this tour. Return to the saddle under Mt. Vígla, cross a roadway and later walk to the left from there, using steps down to the sea. After a few metres along the street, you come to the

1.30   former monastery of **Ayía Triáda** (the Sacred Trinity, built in 1898). In the monastery's atmospheric courtyard paved with pebbles, you can have the church opened up and admire the remarkable icons to the Trinity.

Afterwards, on the cliff in front of the neighbouring monastery of **Áyios Elías** (beside the walled residential

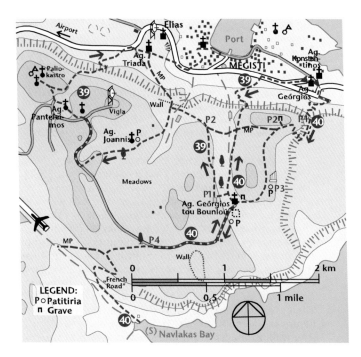

★   houses) built in 1758, you can dream a little before walk-
       ing along the flagstone path, the street and the short-cut
1.40   through the houses to return to the wide **natural har-
       bour.**

⑩ The French Road

This five-hour hike leads to a relic of World War I, past an archaic settlement, and on to the abandoned Monastery of Ayios Geórgios tou Bounioú. With a bit of luck, you will be able to get the keys to the monastery ㉟. Don't forget drinking water and perhaps bathing shoes.

■ *6 km, difference in alt. 210 m, moderate to difficult*

▷ *Map see previous page.*

AWT
0.00 At the **upper town square**, walk uphill between the domed church of Saint George (of the field) and the monument to Déspina, the "country woman of Ro" and then 200 m on the same level as far as the street. Turn up right there and, after 250 m, right again as far as a left turn-off with stop sign. Here you go left for 20 m and find unas-
0.05 suming **stone steps** leading up into rocky terrain. From the lovely stepped path, you see the city of Kas on the
0.15 Turkish coast. After the **last steps** (**P1:** N36°08.706'/ 29°35.753', 125 m), walk straight on with a stone wall on your left.

You wander along a flat stretch for a short while to reach a cistern (right) and, next to it, a winding path up to the right which leads to the plain above. At the top, you see a round structure on the right of the slope. To take a look at
0.35 it, turn off to the right of the main path. This is an **ancient grave** which was used as a shelter by the Italians in the war and now serves as a goat pen (**P2:** N36°08.725'/ E29°35.591', 200 m).

From there, wander back and, on the plateau, to the left
0.45 of the hill, south to the large, round **Cyclopean Walls**
(left). They date back to the 6th century BC and are part of
an archaic settlement. 80 m further, immediately to the
left of the path, is a patitíri (**P3**: N36°08.519'/ E29°
35.556'), an ancient winepress, as described in ㉟. The
0.55 path leads on to the right at the fork, to the **Monastery of
Ayios Geórgios tou Bunioú**, on your left as you pass.
See ㉟.

After finding another patitíri there, 60 m lower down,
walk southwest along the country lane across the high
1.05 plain until you come to a solitary, raised **olive tree** (**P4**:
N36°08.306'/ E29°34.984'). Here you continue to the left
along the "French Road" down into the valley.

> *The French built these well preserved ramps* ① *in World
> War I in order to haul heavy artillery up to the plateau.
> Turkey, at that time allied with Germany, represented a
> threat to France, which needed the island as a stepping
> stone for its Indian possessions.*

1.25 The ramp ends at the **rocky bay of Navlákas** ②, at that
time a landing stage. In a rock pool it is possible, with
some effort, to get straight into the deep water, but it is
wise not to swim out too far.

2.05 Return the same way, only now with **St. George's
Monastery** on the right, and wander straight along a
clearly visible path above a hollow full of trees until you
reach the edge of the cliff. There you will find another
2.25 splendid set of steps down into the village of **Megísti**.

Nísyros

Island connoisseurs swoon when they hear this name mentioned. The volcanic island has hardly any beaches worth mentioning and has thus remained more natural than the surrounding islands. Day-trippers from Kós arrive at 11 am and depart again at 4 pm. Then the island belongs to the locals and their guests once again. You soon come into contact with the people, at the latest in the evening at the romantic main square in Mandráki, the Platía Ilikioméni.

Opening up in the island's interior is a gigantic caldera, or crater which came into being long ago when an immense cavern caved in. The island's rim is formed by a ring of very fertile mountains which are used for agriculture. Many, partly restored, partly dilapidated old mule tracks still exist. You must be careful in the mountains because of the fog and clouds.

In the internet it is possible to download a good hiking map at www.bjfranke.privat.t-online.de for free.

④ On the Volcano

You climb over the edge of the crater on old paths and drop down into the dormant volcano, where you can feel the earth's thin crust and the smell of sulphur tickles your nose. Later, you return along the island's rim.

The six-hour walk can be shortened in the middle, if you manage to arrange a return trip from the crater in the excursion bus with Enetikon Travel (near harbour).

■ *14 km, difference in altitude 325 m, difficult*

AWT If you do not want to take a taxi to the **Monastery of Evangelístria**, you follow the description in ㊷ to get there.

0.50 Leading away to the right from the gigantic **terebinth tree** in front of the monastery (240 m) is a narrow, fenced alleyway ①. At its end, you take a path dropping left and soon come past a cistern. Down on the left lies a deep valley floor, Káto Lákki. Cross the roadway in the hollow and wander uphill along the Profitis Elias massif.

1.15 Walking downhill again, you reach a **pass (P1: N36° 35.840'/ E27°09.720; 325 m)** and, beyond where a path turns off to the right, you see the green plains of the caldera ② beneath you, dominated by the monastery of Ioánnis Theológos on the other side. A wide, very gravelly

1.45 path leads downhill through olive terraces to the **asphalt road** (110 m), which you march along to the right. Up on the right are geothermal drilling rigs. Economic utilisation of terrestrial heat has failed so far due to the popula-

2.05 tion's resistance. The road leads you to the **kiosk** under shady eucalyptus trees.

Till now, you have taken no notice of the main attraction: where lines of tourists disappear and reappear, there is a gigantic, 25 m deep and almost circular hole, Stephen's Crater. As you go down into it, the odour of sulphur from the earth's interior becomes more intensive. At the bottom you sense how the heaving bed is, in some places, only about 20 cm thick. Muddy grey water bubbles underneath. This is the largest of a total of five craters which can be visited. The last time the volcano was active was in 1888. As on Milos und Santorini, the European and African continental plates meet here, which keeps caus-

ing earthquakes. The most recent was in 1933.

Alternative: If you are looking for a nice spot to rest above the caldera ③, walk south-east first, without a path, up to the roadway which leads to the **Stavros Monastery.** From there, walk downhill for five minutes until you reach the portal described at AWT 2.35.

2.05   The continuation initially leads in the same direction along the dusty, white roadway in front of the shady
2.10   roofs, traverses a **farmyard** at the foot of the mountain
2.15   and, behind that, joins an elevated **footpath** (**P2:** N36°34.538'/ E27°09.712'), which runs up into a dry ditch and later meanders through the rocks. Here you need the practised eye of an island hiker to recognise the partially overgrown, romantic trail. Beyond a dilapidated
2.35   portal, take the **sandy road** (**P3:** N36°34.532'/ E27° 09.212'; 240 m) to the right, passing a cave chapel (right) after 300 m. The sandy road leads along above the sea,
2.50   then across a broad green **saddle** (325 m) with the ruins of a hamlet. Later you pass the dilapidated Zacharias chapel (left) and wander on to the north. Out to sea you see Astipálea and other small islets.

Even before the sandy road curves right along the hillside,
!!   you encounter a roadway coming up from a barn. *20 m before it,* at a height of about 5 m, it is possible to discern
3.15   the traces of the old **path** (**P4:** N36°35.484'/ E27°08.361'). Willingly taking it, you later – 10 m further over to the
3.20   right – cross the **sandy road.** Walking on flagstones again, you find a marked left turn-off after four minutes, but this does not lead to a suitable path. So continue straight ahead along the wall-lined path through olive groves until, at a large cistern, you reach the sandy road

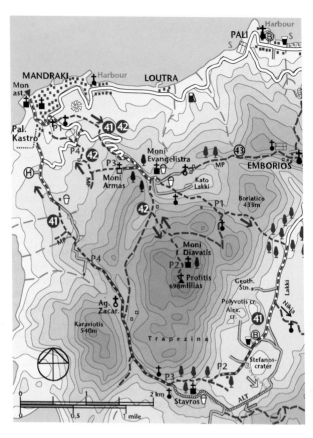

again. Go left up it and, behind the helipad, left again at
3.45 the fork to the **Paleókastro**, the ancient "castle".

> *The reconstructed walls form an obtuse angle and, in the
> 5th and 4th century BC, protected the land side of a lost
> city. The gigantic basalt blocks which were fitted together
> precisely and the well preserved castle gate are most im-
> pressive.*

Next to the little ticket office below the access path to the
3.55 castle gate, a narrow footpath leads down to **Mandráki**.

㊷ The Summit Monastery

This four-to-five-hour tour first leads up to the Evangelístria Monastery, then on along steep mule track to the abandoned little Diavátis Monastery and finally to the summit panorama.

■ *11 km, difference in altitude 700 m, difficult*

▷ *Map see previous page.*

AWT
0.00
0.08

Heading away from the sea, first walk up the alley below the **monastery in Mandráki**, then up the street which gently curves to the left until you come to a **fork**. Continue uphill to the right past the wayside shrine (right) for 60 m and, *30 m before* a chapel, turn left onto a level narrow path ☑ (**P1:** N36°36.568'/ E27°08.060') through care-

0.15

fully laid out horticultural terraces. At the two **forks** you first go right, then left – always uphill. Oaks and fig cacti offer shade along the wonderful, gently ascending path

0.30

☑. You cross the **road** and find the connecting path on the other side right away. You meet it two more times be-

0.40
0.50

fore walking along the **road** to arrive at the **Evangelístria Monastery**, dedicated to the Annunciation. The church possesses a valuable icon. There is a well in the churchyard.

A gigantic tree, a terebinth, stands in front of the cloister. ㊸ turns off here.

!

Walk *60 m back* along the road. A *footpath* marked with red dots turns off to the left here, leading uphill to the south – don't confuse it with the roadway on the left of it!

1.00

It leads leisurely up to a **stable** (left). This is where a wall-

lined mule track starts climbing. (Another one runs right, down into a valley.) The path  rises slowly and later becomes a real delight under shady **kermes oaks.** Ferns line the path up to the wildly romantic **Diavátis Monastery (P2:** N36°35.470'/ E27°09.360', 620 m) situated in a hollow  high above the sea.

1.20
1.40

1.50 The only way up to the chapel of **Profítis Elías** at the peak is along trekking paths between kermes oak bushes. From the survey point (698 m), it is possible to see Kós in the north and, behind it, Kálymnos. In the east is the Turkish peninsula Resadiye, on which the ancient Greek city of Kidnos was located. Tílos is in the south, and, in the west you can see lovely Astipálea. There is still plenty to discover!

You need 1½ hours back to **Mandráki** along the same route (=AWT 3.20).

Another option takes just as long, but requires more path-finding skills:

2.40 300 m after the **Evangelístria Monastery** you go off the road to the left and come to the walled, unoccupied **Armás Monastery (P3:** N36°36.195'/ E27°08.758').

2.50

Below it you continue in the same direction along a trekking path which curves gently to the right. After 300 m, behind walls, a wide, gravelly ramp descends at right angles. Further on, however, you have to search for the continuation on several occasions. A very distinct path first leads to ruins and later to the **road (P4:** N36°36.370'/ E27°08.264').

3.10

On the other side of it you continue using the path or go right along the road, then left down to **Mandráki.**

3.20

㊸ Greek Sauna

From Páli, you walk up to the rim of the crater on a pleasant four-hour hike, wander along the rim and return to Mandráki. In addition, you can discover a natural sauna and a wonderful restaurant on the edge of the volcano!

■ *10 km, difference in alt. 370 m, moderate to difficult*

AWT
0.00
0.05
0.10

At the tranquil fishing harbour of **Páli** you walk inland from the **eastern pier**, turn left with the street and, after 10 m, right ①. The little street climbs slightly and is soon covered in white. If you go left at the fork, you arrive at a building with a terrace in front where the white splendour suddenly ends and a somewhat dilapidated **set of steps** begins. Later leading over scree, it takes you up to the **street**.

Alternative: The way described from this point on requires a certain pioneering spirit as well as long trousers. If you would rather take a more comfortable route, stroll uphill along the street to reach a water collection tank ③ (= AWT 0.35) in less than 25 minutes. The old monopáti continues on the other side of the street – albeit three metres higher up. To reach it, go 50 m left along the street, 3 m up right and then along on the same level until you meet the path again. It is, however, rather overgrown after a few metres, so, for safety's sake, you should use the fence on the left as a guide. When the fence turns off to the left, continue uphill on a mule track and then bear left at the fork. The next destination is a chapel, visible a little higher up on the left ②.

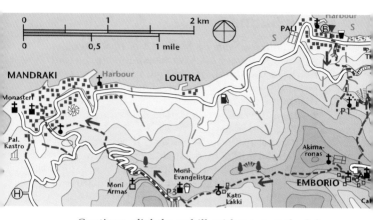

Continue slightly uphill without a path, left across a meadow, then 50 m later through a gully made of pumice-stone and, along narrow paths below the fence,

0.25 up to the picturesque **chapel** (**P1**: N36°36.695'/ E27° 10.475', 150 m). From here you take the new roadway.

0.30 Across a ridge you come to the **asphalt road**, where you

0.35 go right to the roadside **water collection tank** ③ (**P2:** N36° 36.557'/ E27°10.740').

★ On the left side of the tank, a delightful old flagstone path winds its way uphill under oak trees to **Emborió**. There

0.50 you go left along the road and, after 80 m, find the **natural sauna** on the right ④.

The room made of layered stones measures 1.50 x 1.50 m and is hellishly hot. The (apparently mildly radioactive) steam is heat escaping from the earth through the moss-covered stones.

The taverna "Balkóni" located next to the church offers refreshingly cool drinks and delicious food as well as a fantastic view into the volcanic crater.

From the square in front of the taverna are steps leading up to the castle ruins above the ghost village, which was abandoned after the earthquake in 1933. Most of its inhabitants moved down to Páli. In the past few years, however, life has returned to some of the ruins.

Proceeding below the castle (left) on level ground, you come to the upper car park. Directly in front of this you turn left and leave the village through the last ruins paint-

1.00 ed pale blue, below the **upper church** (left). At the steps leading up to the cemetery on the right, you continue on the same level ⑤. Parts of the original path have slipped away, but numerous red markings indicate detours. Be-

1.15 neath the peak, wander past an interesting grey rock formation until you **notice the sea.** Now walking downhill, with a view of Mandráki harbour, you arrive at a plateau

★ with olive trees and oaks under which you can have a splendid rest ⑥. Your eyes rove from the pumice-stone island of Gyáli to the long island of Kós.

The trail continues above the deep valley of Káto Lakki

1.35 (left), traverses a dilapidated **farmyard** and then a narrow pass between two fences before finally arriving at the

1.45 **Evangelístria Monastery**, which is usually locked (**P3:** N36°36.129'/ E27°09.120', 255 m).

At the gigantic terebinth tree, walk along the road until you come to the first sharp right bend. After 10 m you

1.55 find a marked **turn-off** to the left along a footpath. It meets the street twice, crosses it once and finally ends up

2.30 in **Mandráki.**

Psérimos

A tranquil island – when the day-trippers from Kós have set sail again. Scarcely 30 locals and a few soldiers live here. While there are a lot of sometimes rather overpriced tavernas and a sufficient number of beds, there is no shop.
To reach the island, it is best to arrange separate outward and return journeys on excursion boats starting in Kós instead of the "Three Islands Tour".

④ A Dream Beach

This leisurely two-hour hike can be done with ease on a day excursion. It leads to the interior of the island along a country lane and later, along goat tracks, arrives at the long sandy beach next to the chapel of Panagía Grafiótissa.
■ *5 km, difference in altitude 130 m, easy*

AWT	
0.00	The roadway into the interior of the island begins directly at the **harbour** and leads past the tavernas and the church of the Assumption of the Virgin (Panagía), where architectural fragments of the early Christian church can be seen in the forecourt. At the fork in front of a group of
0.06	pines, bear left, and then left again at the **right turn-off** next to the olive groves. Now you can "enjoy" the Greek countryside: walking through a little valley with unimaginative houses and carefully scattered remains of used
0.15	items, you head for a large fenced **shed.**

Alternative: If you go straight ahead on the right of the fence, you find a path over the hilltop, walk across a

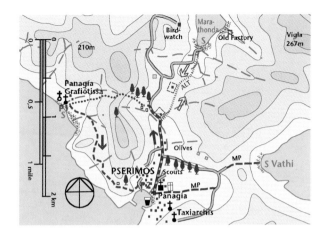

lovely valley floor and arrive after 20 minutes at the **pebble beach of Marathónda**, bordered by greenery. In the next bay are the remains of a brick factory. The new house up on the hill on the left is for watching migratory birds.

From the large shed the roadway climbs to the left. At the **0.20 ruins of a farmstead** you leave the roadway to the left and walk through the ruins. Beyond them you wander, without a path, through the left-hand group of trees and a **0.35** gully, then along comfortable goat paths up to the **saddle** (130 m). The rift remains about 80 m below on the left. From here, you have a view of the islands of Platís and Kálymnos and of the chapel on the beach (photo).

Along goat tracks and also without a path on the left **0.55** above the cleft, you arrive safe and sound at the **Chapel of Panagía Grafiótissa (P1:** N36°56.458'/ E27°07.313'). At the second chapel, you see what happens if you don't build on solid rock. Stretching out down below is a long sandy beach, deserted because the excursion boats cannot land in the shallow water.

Walk back to the village on a distinct path above the shoreline, later on the left of the rocky hill. Shortly before the harbour you see the ruins of a farm on your left, go **1.25** left in front of a fence before sauntering down to the sandy beach of **Psérimos-Chóra (P2:** N36°55.982'/ E27°07.954'). The inn-keepers have been waiting for you!

Sími

The once prosperous city is beginning to blossom again.
Having been left to decay for a long time, tourism has given
it back its distinguished character. Many houses have been
renovated (photo left) and the prices make a pretty picture
too. Primarily British and Scandinavian holidaymakers feel
extremely contented here.

Beyond the colourful harbour village the landscape has plenty
of lovely sights to offer: large monasteries, shady pine forests
and many old mule tracks. While walking, you should take
into account that Sími is hotter than the other islands – especially when it comes to the inclines, which usually have to be
overcome twice over.

④⑤ The Chapel of Áyios Vassílios

*Hidden in the magnificent crags high above the blue
sea is a tiny church. You will discover it in addition
to a broad, deserted bay for swimming. You will
need a total of five hours, a lot of water and perhaps
some food. You walk along monopátia and well-
marked footpaths providing little shade. Due to its
length and, the two ascents of 300 metres in altitude
each, the hike is strenuous.*

*You may be able to pre-arrange the return leg with
an excursion boat.*

■ *12 km, difference in alt. 290 m, moderate to difficult*

AWT 0.00	From the **bridge** you stroll along the southern edge of **Gialós** harbour and, in front of the café Aegialos, take the second alley leading inland, pass the church and its belltower (left) and turn left at the end of the sports field (right). From there, make your way towards the antennas on the peak to the right of the castle hill and, bearing right, find the wide, steep set of stairs that is still in the shadow of the mountain in the morning. The stairs are called Kataráktis – waterfalls – which says everything. At the top, turn right and head for the upper of the two
0.20	churches. At the outer **forecourt** of this church you notice dots marking the way straight ahead, on the same level as the church, and then continue up more steps to the left.
	Soon you leave the houses behind on the left and can enjoy a superb view of the elegant city. Turn right at the
0.25	**fork (P1:** N 36°36.630'/ E27°49.996', 180 m) after the ga-
0.35	te! The delightful, rocky path  leads to the **Chapel of Ayía Paraskeví**, the protectress of eyes. Your first break on the shady dancing area is most welcome.
	From here on the monopáti has been renovated to over-perfection, leading through a sparse little copse of kermes
0.45	oaks to the road. The **Michail Perivilótis Monastery** (285 m) across the way is shut, so proceed to the left.
	At the corner of the entrance to the monastery gardens, immediately turn right onto a concrete path which leads through gardens blessed with numerous chapels. The
0.50	concrete path ends 200 m after the **Áyios Nikoláos Monastery** hidden among trees (right).
	15 m before a gate, follow the coloured dots left. They lead you down towards the sea on the right side of the oc-

✓
★

1.20

casionally steep ravine. Above the sea, you walk through a wildly romantic landscape with sparse woods ② and already pick out the beach. Standing beyond the shady **woods** are ruins (**P2:** N36°35.633'/ E27°48.748', 145 m) on the left of the path, which then makes a left curve towards the sea. Sauntering along above the sparkling blue sea,

1.35

you shouldn't miss the **Chapel of Áyios Vassílios**, St. Blasius ③, below on the right of the path! Steps lead down to a wonderful spot to sit above the sea. The church has old, but unfortunately very sooty frescoes. All the utensils required for a proper church festival are stored in the little building across the way.

The rest of the way to the beach ④ is without a path and

1.45

steep, but not dizzying. Down below on the long **bay** are pebbles and sand and, except when boat parties drop by, not a soul.

2.05
2.35
2.45

Return the same way: past the **ruins**, along the ravine to the **concrete road** and through the fields as far as in front of **Perivilótis Monastery.**

From here you can go down the same way to the right and reach the city in 20 minutes. This is the kalderími with the better view!

If you still fancy a little detour, walk to the left along the

2.55

flat road and turn right at the **concrete road** to arrive at the locked **Fanoúrios Monastery**, where a second

3.30

kalderími leads down to **Gialós.**

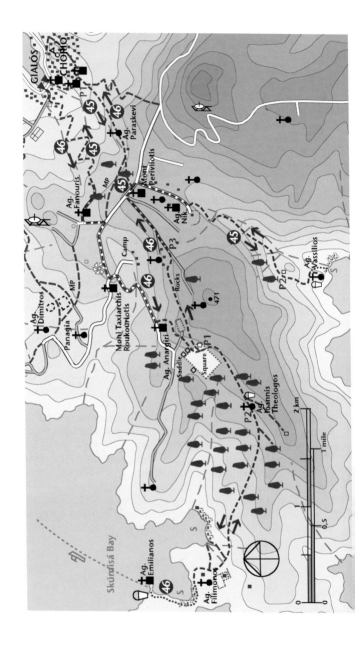

⓸⓺ The Monastery in the sea

For the loveliest walking tour on the island you need eight hours, endurance and plenty of water. Sights include a fortified monastery and, after lengthy yet flat paths through a pine forest, a monastery on an island.
As a short-cut you can try to organise your return on the excursion boat from Áyios Emilianós the evening before in Gialós or take a taxi to Anárgiri.
■ *19 km, difference in altitude 325 m, difficult*

▷ *Map on previous page.*

AWT
0.00

At the **bridge** in **Gialós** harbour the street leads inland on the left of the square. The abandoned barrel-vaulted building with a double nave on the left before the next square is the former ice factory. Before the street climbs (p.162 ⊡), even before the grey water tank, walk up a lane on the left to reach an old kalderími further uphill. This winds its way up - alongside a water pipe, finally on a concrete track – to the small, locked **Monastery of Áyios Fanoúris** (230 m).

0.35

There you first take the concrete track to the left to the road, then go to the right and - in a wide left curve - arrive at the **Monastery of Taxiárchis Micháelis Roukouriótis** ⊡.

0.50

A shrine already stood here in Antiquity. The present monastery from the 15th century has smooth walls on the outside and, inside, a series of terraces laid out around the two-storey katholikón. The upper church has frescoes

of all the saints, and, one by one, they have been "smoked" with incense by the woman who lives in the monastery. The icons and carvings from the 18th century are remarkable. The main attraction is the archangel Michael in embossed silver on the right of the iconostasis. The island's patron saint, he is fighting evil with his sword; in his left hand, he holds a child symbolising the soul.

In the lower church, you also can view frescoes, albeit in poor condition.

Upon leaving the monastery, walk around the tree and down the concrete track. After the military camp (left),

1.00 you quickly come to the charming but locked **Ayíi Anárgiri Monastery.**

Above the monastery walls, red dots draw your attention to an old stone path which is initially flat and later crosses a concrete track at an angle before gradually leading up

1.15 into a saddle (275 m) with three ruins and a **square** mea-

!! suring 60 x 80 m surrounded by stones. *Don't walk straight through the rectangle! The clever hiker turns immediately about 45° to the left* and looks for red markings on the stone wall (**P1: N36°36.288'/ E27°48.205'**). A path me-

1.30 anders right, through a pine forest ②, to the **Áyios Ioánnis Theólogos Chapel** ③ (**P2: N36°35.882'/ E27°47.755',** 260 m) with a cistern. You have already seen your destination down in the water, the monastery in the sea. But first take a short break in front of the chapel!

!! Directly below it, you head downhill. But *two minutes later,* be sure not to miss the path *down to the right.* You are approaching your goal ④.

Down at the bottom, make a wide right curve to the left half way up the slope overlooking the coastal plain and,

2.10	before the fence on the right, proceed up to the **Áyios Filímonos Monastery**. Ask the friendly fisherman who lives there whether you can look at the old frescoes in the tiny barrel-vaulted church.
	Concrete steps lead to the sandy bay with numerous sea-urchins.
2.20	*The **Monastery of Áyios Emilianós** is situated on a rocky offshore island. In the pleasant courtyard, it is easy to imagine spending a few days in a monastery. At the stone table at the tip of the island you can finalise your plans for a different life …*
	But you don't have much time for sitting around today.
3.20	Take the same way back via the **St. John's chapel** to reach
3.35	the **square.**
	Alternative: The rest of the way described below leads through rocks and is fairly difficult. You can take the same return route along the road, only missing the nice view over to the mainland of Asia.
	In the square, follow the markings indicating the way up to the right and then, at about 300 m asl, walk along the slope. If you don't miss any of the red dots in the pointed
4.00	rocks, you arrive at a **farmstead** with a chapel in the saddle (**P3:** N 36°36.281'/ E27°48.968', 315 m). On the far side you take the country lane uphill, then downhill to
4.10	the closed **Perivilótis Monastery.**
	On the other side of the road, another monopáti, 20 m off to the right, leads down into the valley. After passing the
4.15	double chapel of **St. Paraskeví**, being sure to beseech her
★	for good eyesight, you behold the beautiful sight of Sími.
4.35	The upper part, **Chorió**, is soon reached.
	Depending on the amount of energy you still have left, you can take the steep staircase (kataráktis) on the left before the kástro down to Gialós or the longer but nicer Kalí Stráta ("Good Street") to the harbour. Phew!

▶ **Short walking tour on a day excursion:**
Follow the above description up to **Fanoúris Monastery**, go left along the concrete track as far as the **main road**, later turning left at **Perivilotis Monastery** (right) (AWT 4.10). A monopáti brings you past the church of **Ayía Paraskeví** and then back to the harbour with a beautiful view. Total time: 1½ to 2 hours.

㊼ Around Emborió

It takes four hours to discover the hilly northern part of Sími. The paths are easy to find, the inclines are slight and there is a place to stop off for a swim and refreshments, as well as a boat for the return journey – but no fountains.

■ *10 km, difference in altitude 135 m, moderate*

AWT 0.00	At the **bridge in Giálos**, walk inland past the taverna Vasilis on the left and with a square on the right. Turn slightly to the right, pass the old barrel-vaulted ice factory and then march up the street ① to the right. The grey water tank is down on the left.
0.10	20 m after the **cemetery** (left), turn onto a footpath to the left. It is marked in blue and red and mounts in a curve to
0.20 !!	the right. After a gate, you pass a **house** (right) and look down upon the bay of Emborió ②. From there you do *not descend,* but proceed half way up the hillside along goat tracks in a sweeping curve above first the sea, then a wide
0.45	valley on the right. Above the long **fence** you come across a path (**P1**: N36°37.082′/ E27°48.897′, 120 m).
0.50 !!	Pay attention about 50 m after the **ridge** – be sure not to overlook the indistinct *turn-off down to the right!* In front of a wire mesh fence it leads downhill and then between
0.55	two walled **gardens**, where an ancient patitíri was hewn into the bedrock – a round winepress (p. 139 ③). In the dip you go to the right in front of the wall through a dry
1.00	stream bed and up to **Áyios Dimítrios chapel**.

Directly after the chapel, leave the street downhill towards the right and turn to the left 40 m afterwards in or-

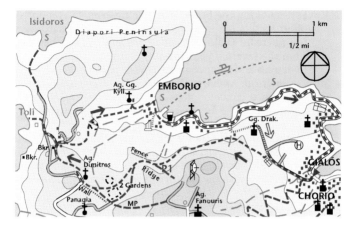

der to arrive at the next hilltop with the roadway. Walk
1.05 along it to the right until it forks after the **bunker** on the
left.

> *Alternative:* Below the left roadway is a path which
> runs down the pebble beach of **Tolí** (15 minutes, see
> map).

Walk a few metres to the right along the country lane towards Emborió and, at a new house, take the footpath to
the right down into the valley. On the right of the path
are field walls and fences. After passing through a gate,
proceed to the left almost horizontally 60 m above a
sharp incision in the terrain and then, for the sake of the
view, a few metres uphill to the closed chapel of Áyios
Geórgios Kylindriotis.

From there, descend through the boulders to the wide
1.35 **Emborió bay** and to the right along the beach.

> *If you follow the dry stream bed inland after 100 m, you
> arrive at the only interesting sight. 80 m away from the
> sea, turn off to the left to ascend steps to an early Christ-
> ian basilica. To the right of it are Roman-early Christian
> mosaics.*
>
> *If you continue in this direction, above the cemetery,
> coloured markings lead to twelve subterranean vaults,
> called "Dódeka Spília". A secret school for painting icons
> is said to have existed here in the Turkish era. But they
> could also be early Christian tombs.*

1.40   Further along the beach, the nice **taverna** "Metapontis" offers seaside life in a confined space. A taxi-boat leaves from here for Gialós at 4 pm, 5 pm and 6 pm. Otherwise, from the taverna, you continue along the concrete track by the sea and soon come to a sandy beach.

1.50   *Short-cut:* After a **wall made of quarry stone** (right), marked concrete steps turn off uphill on the right. Walk past the Áyios Geórgios Drakoundiótis Monastery to reach **Gialós** in about 25 minutes.

The concrete track along the seaside is much nicer. With the sea on your left, stroll along and enjoy the grand finale. With the sun astern, navigate into the harbour and

2.15   anchor at one of the restaurants in **Gialós**.

Tílos

The traveller is greeted by the wide bay around the harbour town of Livádia. Here the softly modelled island shows hardly any rough cliffs, only several green areas. A pleasant, tranquil kind of tourism is celebrated here. Not only most of the individual travellers come from England, but also a precise map of the island, which can be purchased in the shops. The numerous springs are very useful during the walking tours.
Walks 42 and 43 lead along restored paths.

㊽ Mikró Chório

Mikró Chorió means "small village". Actually it is more a small town, which however has not been inhabited since 1967 and has since fallen into disrepair. It is the first destination on this five-hour walk along mule tracks, which then leads through a romantic ravine to the sea and returns, high above the coast, to Livádia. That is where the inhabitants of Mikró Chorió headed for, too, in those days.

■ *9 km, difference in altitude 210 m, moderate*

AWT 0.00   In **Livádia**, go up the old path with steps on the right of the **taverna "Omónoia"** ("Harmony"). Still in Livádia, it soon becomes a footpath before it meets up with a road at the top. Follow the road to the left. 50 m *before* the main road are steps and a **gate**, which you pass through in order to wander further along the old path. Open and shut a second gate before you arrive at the beautiful old mo-

0.07

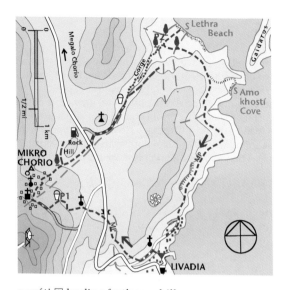

nopáti ① leading further uphill.

0.17 At a culvert you cross the **street** and, a little later, a newer
0.20 **concrete track.** Immediately after it, follow the wall (chapel right), then turning off to the left. Later you walk right, between level terrace walls, and pass the old (dry) spring house with a triangular superstructure (**P1**: N36° 25.318'/ E27°22.514'). Crumbling walls alongside olive terraces gradually get you in the mood for the ghost town. Climbing up the rift, you come to a roadway and walk up
0.40 a few steps to a closed **disco.** The youth of the island meets here amid the ruins in July and August.

The largest of the churches in the abandoned village of **Mikró Chorió** ② has been renovated. The smaller one below the castle has very old frescoes. You look at the saints eyeball to eyeball – assuming divine providence grants you entrance. Strolling through the narrow lanes, up and down the steps, is quite an experience.

After exploring, walk down the lane in front of the church, past two superimposed chapels (left) and, after

!!
0.50

100 m, *to the left* towards the sea at a fork (left house with wooden door lintel). After the **last ruins**, you walk along the foot of the mountain, still ahead of a rocky hill, walk straight on at a big kermes oak, leaving the rocks on your left. Walking in or next to a dry stream bed, you arrive at

1.00

the **street**.

Go through a gate on the other side of the street and walk downhill along a new lane. Continue uphill to the right

1.05
!!
★
1.30

at a nice walled **fountain** ③. At the *cairns 60 m later,* plunge down *to the left* into a wildly romantic ravine. Hopping between oleanders and boulders, you arrive on the plain with **Léthra Bay**.

If you find the pebbles too big and the (few) other swimmers too many, you can pick out another place to swim further on. You walk back to the ravine in five minutes

1.35

and turn uphill to the left at the **fork** marked by thick cairns (**P2**: N36°26.177'/ E27°23.130'). When you see the Bay of Livádia again, thinner cairns point out that you go downhill there for eight minutes to reach **Amokhosti Bay.** You are usually alone here.

2.20

Return to **Livádia** along a wonderful coast path ④, bearing left when you reach the edge of the village.

⑭ Neró

Water, "neró" in Greek, is only available in cisterns on many islands. On this impressive hike, however, you pass no fewer than three springs whose cool water you can drink.
The tour takes five to six hours and mostly follows old paths. One short descent without a path requires sure-footedness.
■ *15 km, difference in alt. 275 m, moderate to difficult*

AWT 0.00	From the Italian **harbour building** in **Livádia**, saunter along the paralía past the hotels and eateries. When you have circled the bay, turn right onto a road leading uphill in front of the taverna "Fáros" at the fishing harbour of
0.30	**Áyios Stéfanos.** Where the asphalt surfacing ends, you
0.45	are greeted by the **Chapel of St. John** ① and guided by a renovated kalderími ②. The hikers' prayers have evidently
★	been heard by the authorities. As you walk uphill, don't
!!	forget to look back! (p. 165). Proceed on the right of a rift
1.00	with oleander as far as a **fork**, *20 m ahead of a small bridge* (**P1:** N36°24.467'/ E27°24.760'). Turn left there, pass a di-
!!	lapidated farm after the oleander rift and later be careful
1.15	not to miss the left **turn-off** ③ (**P2:** N36°24.167'/ E27°25.190', 125 m).

Alternative: If you continue straight on for ten minutes, you come to the impressive village in ruins called Ierá, where only goats and ghosts still reside. The last families moved away around 1960.

Red markings help along the way down to the water, so
1.30   you soon reach the **well**. It is said that water was found

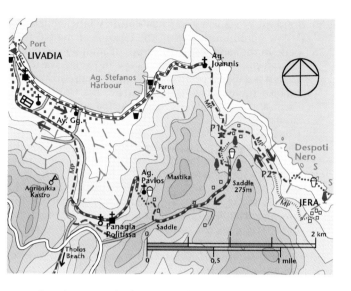

here by a priestly dignitary who was almost dying of thirst after a sea voyage. That is why this region is called Despóti Neró. There are two beaches here. The hot black pebbles would certainly cause Indian fire-walkers hellish joy. The rest of us must first use cool sea water from a plastic bag to be able to sit and enjoy the great view of the Turkish peninsula Resadyie.

2.05 Return the same way to the **oleander rift.**

Walk uphill to the left along the rift to arrive at a walled grove guarded by cairns and go round it to the right. A few metres further down is another (fenced) spring. Be-

2.20   hind the grove you join a new **country lane**, which you
       follow uphill on the left of the remains of the old foot-
2.25   path. In the **saddle** (with the ruins of a house) you have a
       view over a gently rolling landscape and a new waste col-
       lection point on a peninsula. While it is praiseworthy that
       rubbish should no longer be burned, the Greeks of the
       classical period would have constructed a temple on this
       sublime spot.

       Continue along the hillside lane, below which runs the
       old flagstone path, on the same level until you reach the
2.35   next **saddle.** From here you see the Bay of Livádia again
       and leave the lane to the right. On the right at the same
       level are a few dilapidated houses which can be reached
2.40   quickly along a goat path. At the trees in the **second
       group of houses**, a red marking indicates the beginning
       of the steep descent without a path across grazing mead-
       ows and rocks. Soon a large pine and the idyllically
2.50   situated **Chapel of Áyios Pávlos** come into view down
       below ④.

           *Inside it is not so much the few icons which are of interest
           as the next spring with fresh water. Outside is a magnifi-
           cent picnic spot.*

       The roadway which commences down below leads to the
       closed **Monastery of Panagía Polítissa.** On only one day
       in the year, on 22 August (Panigíri), is all hell let loose, so
3.10   to speak. Continue on to the **fork**, where you go up left
!!   for a bit, turn *right in the bend* and walk home along the
       old mule track, of course – after all, you are a hiker.
3.35   **Livádia** is reached without any difficulty.

The way to lovely Thólos beach:
From Livádia, first take the way described directly above
and then walk up the roadway west of Panagía Polítissa
and down the rocky path on the other side of the ridge.
See the map.

㊿ Áyios Panteleímonas

The destination on this four to five-hour hike through the lonely northwest of the island is a romantic monastery with a spring beneath shady trees. To begin with, the route follows a restored mule track, later a marked goat track through the phrygána and finally a fairly long stretch on the road. A short passage in scree might cause a certain dizziness.

■ *7 km, difference in altitude 265 m, moderate*

AWT	
0.00	Having taken the bus to **Áyios António**, walk westwards along the asphalt road, then along a roadway, to reach the
0.20	**Kamariání Monastery**, located in a well tended garden. 40 m after the garden walls, a footpath marked in red leads uphill to the left and, after 30 m, on the same level to the right. The restored footpath initially passes
0.30	through olive terraces ①, then leads past a **cistern** from 1957 (**P1: N 36°27.406'/ E 27°18.833'**) and lovely picnic spots beneath olive trees. Now you have to pay careful at-
0.40	tention: on the former terraces **red arrows (P2: N36°27.594'/ E27°18.602', 130 m)** point *uphill to the left.*
!!	After the ascent you only have to climb slightly to the
0.50	right below a **rock face** until you reach the lonely saddle
1.00	② with the **ruins of a chapel (P3: N 36°27.325'/ E27° 18.229', 265 m)**, whose most valuable feature is the door lintel.

The way down leads along the island's harsh exterior, at times on the old steps. At the beginning those who suffer from vertigo should perhaps busy themselves more with

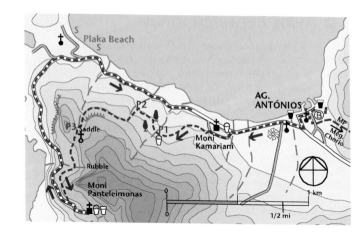

the vegetation on the left rather than look down at the
sea. After a field of scree the widened path continues safe-
1.20 ly through bushes to the **road** and on to the hidden
1.25 **Monastery of St. Panteleímonas.** The shady café there is
a popular place to enjoy the sunset.

> *The picturesque monastery from the 14th century was in-
> habited until 1930, after which it was in danger of
> falling into disrepair. Now freshly renovated, it presents
> itself as a castle keep, cell tract with arcades and Byzan-
> tine katholikón, where the carvings on the iconostasis
> cast a spell on the beholder.*

It is easier and more refreshing to return on the road by
the sea. Especially if you have remembered your swimming things. These are certainly needed if you drop down
2.00 from the **turn-off** to **Pláka beach** in five minutes.

Continue along the road by the sea, at the windmill di-
2.35 rectly on the shore, to **Áyios António.**

Some Greek words for hikers:

Stress on the accents.

jássas	hello	kerós	**weather**
ne	yes	aéras	wind
óchi	no	meltémi	strong north wind
parakaló	please	ílios	sun
efcharistó	thank you	wrochí	rain
endáxi	okay	omíchli	fog
sto kaló	all the best		
kalá	lovely	níssos	**island**
símera	today	farángi, langádi	ravine, gorge
ávrio	tomorrow	kámpos, pláka	plains
pósin óra?	How long?	livádi	meadow
pósso makriá	How far is it to...?	déndro	tree
ine ja?		léfkes	poplars
puíne...?	Where is...?	dássos	forest
óra	hour	lófos	hill
neró	water	wounó, óros	mountain
psomí	bread	vígla	mountain peak
tirí	cheese	vráches	rock, cliff
míkro	small	spíleo	cave
mégalo	big	thálassa	sea
leoforió	bus	órmos	bay
stásis	bus stop	límni	lake
enikáso	rent	potámi	river
aftókinito	auto	réma	dry bed
mechanáki	motor bike	pigí	spring
podílato	bicycle	pérazma	pass, ridge
kaíki	boat	xirolithía	dry wall
hora	**city**	odiporió	**wandering**
horio	hamlet	isía	straight on
spíti	house	dexiá	right
platía	square	aristerá	left
parélia	harbour promenade	apáno	uphill
kástro	Venetian castle	káto	downhill
pírgos	fortified Venetian castle	kondá	near
		makriá	far
nekrotafío	cemetery	ásfalto	asphalt street
limáni	harbour	drómos	street
vrísi	fountain	chomaódromos	gravel street
stérna	cistern	dasikí odós	forest path
kafenío	café, and how!	odós	path
		skála	path of steps
eklisiá	**church**	monopáti	mule track
papás	priest	kalderími	paved way
moní, monastíri	monastery	katsikó drómos	goat path
ksoklísi	chapel	yéfira	bridge
panagía	Mother of God	stavrodrómi	crossing, intersection
panigíri	parish fair		
áyios, ayía, Ay.	saint	hártis	map
ikonostasio	icon altar screen	kutrúmbulo	path marking
katholikón	central building in a monastery	phrýgana	scrub, the island hiker's enemy

Island Hopping

The nicest way to discover the Greek islands is certainly by approaching them from the sea. With the many connections by ship, it is easy to drift from island to island. Boarding and going ashore with almost all of the island's inhabitants taking part is a special experience. Strong winds however, can whirl the ferry schedules into disorder, so chance easily joins you as a travelling companion on this kind of trip.

The **big ferries** are the most pleasant, with their large upper deck which is usually used by tourists. The locals can usually be seen in the salons and restaurants on the lower deck. The reasonable prices are strongly subsidized.

In addition, there are smaller ships for lateral connections and the fast **airfoil boats** and **catamarans.** Unfortunately, you cannot sit outside on the latter and see very little of the sea through the salt-encrusted windows. You pay about double the price for this.

The **main route** for the big ferries, often with several daily trips, goes between **Rhodes,** (not always to **Sími**), **Tílos, Nísyros, Kós** to Kálymnos, and then leads to Piräus via the Cycladian island of Amorgós.

Kárpathos along with **Kássos** and **Chálki** can only be reached from Rhodes, Santorini or Crete. This line goes to Piräus via Mílos. **Chálki** also has a small ferry connection to the harbour of Kámiros-Skála on Rhodes, across from it.

Kastellórizo is linked with Rhodes by ship connection.

The daily excursion boats from **Kós** to **Nísyros** also leave from the harbours of Kamári and Kardámena on Kós.

Small daily ships leave the harbour of Mastichári near the airport on **Kós** for **Kálymnos.**

Psérimos can be reached most easily on the excursion boats from Kós and Kálymnos.

There are several excursion boats daily from Rhodes to **Sími.**

Information on sea connections may be found on the internet at **www.gtpnet.com.**

Abbreviations, Key

▬▬▬▬	hiking route on a road or dirt track
▬▬▬▬	hiking route on a street
━ ━ ━ ━ ·	hiking route on a path
·············	hiking route without a path
·······ᴬᴸᵀ∘∘∘∘∘	alternative route, short-cut
← ⇐	walking direction / alternative
	GPS point
═══════	street
▭▭▭▭	dirt track, sandy track
MP □	monopáti, mule track / marking
━ ━ ━	dry stream-bed (at times), hollow
⍦	antenna
⊕ ⊕'	bus stop / seasonal
Ⓟ	parking area
Ⓗ	helicopter landing pad
⊞	cemetery
+	wayside shrine, monument
⬯	sports field
∩	cave
♪⚔	medieval castle, dwelling tower / ruins
⬠	ancient ruins, statue
·· □	houses / ruins
⚏ ⚎	monastery, large church / ruins
⚏⚏ ⚎	chapel / summit chapel / ruins
▼ ⊟	taverna / open seasonally
✳☼	windmill/watermill, ruins
⌷□ □	fountain, well, spring, reservoir, cistern
S	swimming possible

In the text:

!!	pay attention to turn-off!
↙	possible feelings of vertigo
OW	time for walking one way
★	the author's 20 favourite spots